The Computer Professional's Guide to Effective Communications

Other McGraw-Hill Books of Interest

AUTHOR	TITLE	ISBN
Simon	*How to Be a Successful Computer Consultant, 2/e*	0-07-057554-1 (hard) 0-07-057552-5 (pbk.)
Simon	*The Computer Professional's Survival Guide*	0-07-057574-6
Singer	*McGraw-Hill Guide to Effective Communications for MIS Professionals, 2/e*	0-07-057562-2
Vassiliou and Orenstein	*The Computer Professional's Quick Reference*	0-07-067211-3 (hard) 0-07-067212-1 (pbk.)

To order, or to receive additional information on these or any other McGraw-Hill titles, please call 1-800-822-8158.

MH92

The Computer Professional's Guide to Effective Communications

Alan R. Simon

Jordan S. Simon

McGraw-Hill, Inc.

New York St. Louis San Francisco Auckland Bogotá
Caracas Lisbon London Madrid Mexico Milan
Montreal New Delhi Paris San Juan São Paulo
Singapore Sydney Tokyo Toronto

Library of Congress Cataloging-in-Publication Data

Simon, Alan R.
    The computer professional's guide to effective communications /
Alan R. Simon, Jordan S. Simon.
        p.   cm.
    Includes index.
    ISBN 0-07-057596-7 (hard)—ISBN 0-07-057597-5 (pbk.)
    1. Business communication.   2. Business writing.   3. Technical
writing.   4. Electronic data processing consultants.   I. Simon,
Jordan S.   II. Title.
    HF5718.S548   1993
    808'.066004—dc20   92-23178
                                                                    CIP

HF
5718
5548
1993

1 2 3 4 5 6 7 8 9 0   DOC/DOC   9 8 7 6 5 4 3 2

ISBN 0-07-057596-7 {HC}
ISBN 0-07-057597-5 {PBK}

*The sponsoring editor for this book was Jeanne Glasser, the editing
supervisor was Stephen M. Smith, and the production supervisor was
Suzanne W. Babeuf. It was set in Century Schoolbook by Carol
Woolverton, Lexington, Massachusetts, in cooperation with Warren
Publishing Services.*

Printed and bound by R. R. Donnelley & Sons Company.

Contents

Part 2   Effective Verbal Communication Skills for the Computer Field

Preface

This book is intended to provide the finishing touches to the series of computer-career-oriented books by Alan R. Simon, which began when the first edition of *How to Be a Successful Computer Consultant* was published in 1985. The second edition followed five years later, and was joined shortly thereafter by *The Computer Professional's Survival Guide*. This book explores a subject discussed briefly in each of the previous books—written and verbal communications by computer professionals—in more detail. As we note in Chap. 1 and at various points throughout the book, written and verbal communications skills are just as important an aspect of career success in the computer profession as they are in other career areas. These skills have become even more critical in recent years with massive layoffs and restructurings in the computer industry (a subject explored in *The Computer Professional's Survival Guide*). The ability to differentiate oneself from others is critical not only for career success but for career survival, and one of those differentiators is the ability to successfully communicate one's ideas. For those with aspirations in computer consulting, written and verbal communications skills often mean the difference between winning and losing business opportunities.

We believe that we have provided a concise, consolidated reference for nearly all of the types of written and verbal communications one might encounter during a career in the computer profession. Not only have we dealt with the "standard" types of written material—documentation, proposals, and requirements documents, to name a few—but we have also included a chapter about writing books, articles, and technical papers (an important way to distinguish oneself among peers, and therefore enhance career success possibilities), as well as a chapter on writing product development support documents such as marketing plans. Most computer professionals, as they progress in their careers, find themselves in situations where authorship of documents—or presentation of various verbal information—is required. We hope that the guidelines and examples included in this book will provide guidance. We also have included excerpts from many of the document types. None is intended to represent a complete document, but rather to provide samples of format and content.

Nearly all companies and products referenced in sample business plans, proposals, and other documents, such as LookAtMe windowing software, AllCASE Inc., and Monolithic Computers, are fictional, and no inference should be made as to any real-life product or company. The only exceptions to this are passing references to such common products as MS-DOS and Novell NetWare in the sample documents.

We would like to thank various friends and business associates for lending their names to our sample documents and other material contained in this book. Most of all, we would like to thank our parents, Bernard and Sandra Simon, for their unconditional support and love throughout our respective careers.

Alan R. Simon
Jordan S. Simon

Effective Written Communication Skills for the Computer Field

Overview of
Written Communications

Introduction

Effective written and verbal communications skills are one of the most important attributes for any computer professional's career progression. Without these skills, advancement to the top of today's computer industry is difficult, if not impossible.

The above is not an overstatement. Nearly everyone involved in the computer industry realizes that the days of uncommunicative "computer experts"—the once-popular stereotype of programmers as the industry's form of mad scientists—are rapidly fading into the past. The appearance of computer hardware and software power in nearly every home and business, brought about by the microcomputer revolution, has placed many of the skills (especially software development skills) once reserved only for computer scientists, in the hands of most of the world's general populace. Additionally, this trend will likely accelerate as technologies and methods such as object-oriented programming place advanced coding abilities within the reach of even more people.

Given this trend, it is no longer enough for a computer professional to be a brilliant software developer, or for a hardware designer to be a talented computer architect, to reach the upper tiers of the industry. As the skill set that formerly was held by a relatively small number of computer professionals is acquired by many, differentiators are needed to distinguish one's ability and, more important for those in corporate environments, promotability, in a flattening or even shrinking number of management and executive positions. Even those who turn their backs on the corporate environment and embark on independent consulting or contract work within the computer profession still must be evaluated against a growing number of competitors. The same differentiators apply.

In this book, we will take a detailed look at the written and verbal communications skills computer professionals need. More specifically, the first part of the book provides a concise reference source for most of the types of documents computer professionals encounter as they progress through their careers, with guidelines, tips, and examples. The second part of this book discusses verbal communications, including basic speaking skills, how to teach various types of technical classes, and how to prepare effective presentation materials.

Before we embark on the first part of this book, let's take a brief look at written communications and how the subject applies to computer professionals.

Written Communications

Many college and university students majoring in a computer-oriented program, particularly computer science or computer engineering, receive little formal instruction in written communications other than an introductory course or two in freshman composition. Even the writing taught in computer courses, usually consisting of simplified design documents or code documentation, provides little useful background for the myriad of documents computer professionals will be called upon to write.

While some business-oriented information systems programs such as management information systems (MIS) or computer information systems (CIS) attempt to include courses in business communications in their curricula, these classes usually concentrate on how to write different types of business letters, a topic we cover in just a single chapter in this book (Chap. 11). Given the rest of the material within these pages, it is obvious that further direction is required in composing successful written communications in these other areas.

Communications skills are needed not only by product managers, software marketing managers, development supervisors, or others in positions where great amounts of written communications are required for their primary job functions; even system programmers, software engineers, and other hands-on, development-oriented professionals now find themselves having to write more than they did in years past. There are several reasons for this (see Fig. 1.1), all of which result in the need for this book.

First, consolidation in the computer industry has broken many of the barriers between job functions as the survivors of layoffs and other downsizings are forced to assume more and more roles. In the past, a systems programmer who developed database management system

1. Downsizings and
   Industry Changes

2. Increased Complexity
   of Software

3. Increased Number of
   Intercompany Efforts

Figure 1.1   Reasons for increased importance of written communications.

software for a major hardware vendor may have had little interaction with users, and was able to concentrate on designing and developing DBMS software; the elimination of many customer-oriented positions now has forced those responsibilities on many of the former "I only write code" developers. These people now find themselves writing letters or sending electronic mail memos to users outside of their companies for a number of reasons, which include confirming briefings and meetings and discussing technical issues. Those who formerly relied on secretarial support for these functions now find greatly diminished support on that front, forcing communications functions into their own areas of responsibility.

A second trend is the growing complexity of most software. Applications, for the most part, have always been complex to some degree. System software, such as operating systems, database management systems, compilers, and dictionaries, however, traditionally have operated in something of a vacuum. The software was written for use by other programmers and computer professionals, so documentation did not have to be of the degree required for users of applications. Additionally, the centralized nature of most of the system software alleviated the need for a large number of open, published interfaces with other software, and for the documentation of those interfaces. The trend toward complex software, particularly in distributed, heterogeneous environments, has forced more attention on architectural interface documents, specifications, design documents, and other written communications that traditionally were neglected or ignored by many involved in software development. Given the downsizing trend discussed above, this increased importance has come about at a time of decreased professional writing assistance in most organizations; the result has been that the computer professionals themselves must assume much of this responsibility.

The growing trend toward intercompany joint efforts that took hold with the personal computer era and greatly accelerated at the beginning of the 1990s is the third reason we need higher quality written communications. The industry today is rife with cooperative development efforts, consortia, standards committees, and other areas where members of multiple companies must work together to compete effectively in the marketplace. As hardware and software grow more complex, well-documented requirements, specifications, architectures, and designs (among others) are needed to ensure that distributed teams, often geographically disbursed and usually working for different companies or organizations, can work together effectively in a constrained environment.

Additionally, business letters and memorandums among members of development teams from different companies require a higher level of diplomacy than was necessary in intracorporate environments. That is, a memo beginning with "Hey, you stupid #%$^&" is never the best choice to express displeasure, but is likely to create the intercorporate parallel to an international incident if sent to someone from a company other than the sender's, even if the two individuals are peers working on the same project. In a single-company setting, such a breach of diplomacy might have been handled without involving senior management and damage control specialists.

Types of Written Communications
for Computer Professionals

In this section, we'll look briefly at the types of written communications computer professionals are likely to encounter. Most of them are discussed in further detail in the following chapters, and examples are presented for most.

An important caveat to remember is that in many situations the formal distinctions between some of these types of documents (for example, a system specification and a conceptual design document) may be blurred or eliminated for reasons such as the scale of the system being developed. (The smaller the system and the fewer number of people involved, the less the stepwise refinement between documents might be.) The document types discussed below and in the succeeding chapters are not meant to be inflexible guidelines. For example, a small-scale system might have a combined requirements-specification document with elements from both life cycle phases included, and a feasibility study might be included in the requirements document. Other document types, such as proposals and business plans, sit outside the development life cycle and serve their own purposes. *The important thing to remember is to be flexible with respect to written communications and to choose the type of document most appropriate for the particular situ-*

ation. More importantly, everything written should be of the highest quality possible.

Requirements analysis documents

Most computer systems, particularly those large in scope (numbers of users, lines of code, and other factors) begin with a requirements analysis document. The requirements analysis process traditionally appears at the beginning of the software or system development life cycle (see Fig. 1.2), where "user needs are translated into the requirements of the computer system" (or some other standard, colorless version of that phase). In reality, the requirements analysis process should be one of the, if not *the,* most critical parts of the development life cycle. It is here that the person or team charged with preparing the requirements analysis document must differentiate between true user *needs* and the inevitable wish list of features that appears during the analysis process. Once true needs are established, these must in turn be prioritized based on precedence matrices and other tools that help establish the order in which the resulting system features are developed.

With respect to this book, we are not interested so much in the requirements process itself but rather how to develop high-quality requirements documents. In many circumstances, particularly in governmental and large organization settings, there is a formal set of procedures and formats that guides (or greatly restricts, depending on the quality of the guidelines) the creation of the requirements document. In other cases, the document preparer has a free hand in creating the style and contents of the requirements analysis documents. In Chap. 2, we'll look at requirements documents in detail.

Specifications

Requirements analysis documents ideally should deal with the requirements themselves, not the implementation methods of those re-

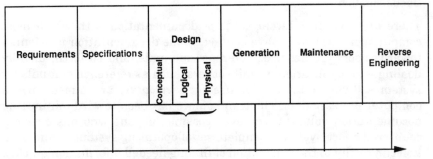

Figure 1.2 The development life cycle.

quirements. Specifications documents take those requirements *that will make their way into the particular system under development* and "computerize" those requirements. Remember that requirements documents include prioritization of features and components, not all of which may be included in the system or software that will be developed initially. That is, the requirement for "user displays" may be refined in a specification document to "displays using a graphical user interface (GUI) platform." Similarly, a requirement for "a global database of customer information" may now be specified as "a distributed database across multiple user nodes."

Feasibility studies

While the requirements analysis process and the resulting documents attempt to determine needs and their priorities, organizations must still determine whether even the most urgently needed system can feasibly be procured or built. Factors such as costs and budgets, technical feasibility, development or procurement tradeoffs, and other elements must be carefully analyzed, and decisions made based primarily (but not solely, since political and other issues also factor into the decision-making process) on the feasibility process. The associated feasibility study documents should carefully document the entire analysis and study process. This area can be hazardous for computer professionals, since competition for ever-dwindling resources is more intense than ever. Consequently, computer professionals charged with preparing feasibility study documents often find themselves drawn into the crossfire between managers and others whose career aspirations—or even survival—depend on the acceptance of a particular development or procurement program. The resulting pressure could include attempts to discredit any feasibility study document (and its author) that may recommend against proceeding with a particular project upon which such career goals are based.

Documentation

There are several different types of documentation with which most computer professionals have contact. Some documentation is oriented towards users (guidebooks, reference manuals, and so forth, usually dealing with applications), while others (such as reference manuals for system software intended for use by developers) are aimed toward computer professionals. The trend of late has been toward minimizing documentation volumes wherever possible; anyone who has ever encountered a forty-volume complete set of operating system documentation can testify to the frustration of finding needed information quickly.

While user-oriented documentation can be minimized through the use of online help and graphical user interfaces (which tend to be self-explanatory) the rise in heterogeneous distributed computing, with its bridges, gateways, and other interfaces, will most likely continue the trend in complicated developer-oriented documentation.

Requests for proposals (RFPs)

RFPs are the mechanism through which organizations solicit proposals from vendors, contractors, and others competitively. Some RFPs, such as those submitted by government organizations, set extremely strict guidelines with respect to the contents, formats, and other aspects of the documents. Others, such as those produced by private organizations may be more lenient in the format requirements. Regardless of the source and governing rules, an RFP should be developed in such a manner that there is little room for dispute regarding the performance of the party submitting the selected proposal. This is accomplished through correct wording, completeness in the items, and other factors discussed in Chap. 6.

Proposals

Proposals can be the lifeblood of a computer professional's career, whether the professional is self-employed (and thus attempting to win business) or works for a large corporation or other type of organization. There are many different types of proposals, each suited to a different goal. Some are developed in direct response to a particular RFP, while others may be unsolicited. Some may be to initiate a development program in a particular area, while others are aimed at other facets of business operations.

Business plans

Business plans are critical for a number of reasons. They are the primary source through which companies, both new and ongoing, request equity and/or debt financing from venture capital firms, banks, and other sources. In other circumstances, business plans serve as the primary focus around which all plans for a specific program or an organization as a whole are coordinated. Business plans may be relatively modest and informal, such as those intended for a solo consulting operation, or long and comprehensive, as when financing is being requested.

Product development support documents

Those computer professionals who work with vendors are likely to be tasked with developing one or more of the support documents that accompany product development efforts. Marketing plans, staffing plans, legal protection strategies, and others are important documents that can have a critical role in the success of any product. Without appropriate legal protection and marketing strategies, for example, even the most inventive software product may have an extremely difficult time becoming a winner in the marketplace.

Professional writing

Many computer professionals supplement their primary job functions by writing articles, technical papers, and books. The kind, intended audience, and other aspects of these publications should be chosen carefully to maximize their benefit.

Business letters

Nearly everyone must write business letters to cover a variety of situations. Careful selection of wording and other aspects of effective business letters are very important in achieving the goal of any letter or memorandum.

Guidelines in Written Communications

There are several guidelines that are appropriate for any of the above-mentioned document types. Whether you are writing a business plan or a requirements document, you should always:

1. *Tailor the document to the particular situation, if allowed.* Unless you are bound by specific corporate or governmental guidelines with respect to the format of a given document, you should always evaluate each situation and adjust such factors as document length, style, formality, and so forth.

2. *Use correct grammar.* Regardless of the language in which the document is being written, it should use correct spelling and grammar.

3. *Use figures, diagrams, and charts where appropriate.* We don't want to use cliches, so we won't say that a picture is worth a thousand words. We will, however, say that the more professional looking your documents are, the more receptive the reader(s) will be to the message they contain. The relatively inexpensive combination

of laser printers and cut-and-paste graphics for word processing documents provides this capability to even solo practitioners in the consulting world.

4. *Remember that form does not make up for bad content.* That is, the most attractive document produced on a laser printer with outstanding graphics is not likely to win business or perform its desired task if the content is lacking. Proposals, business plans, and the other documents discussed above and in the following chapters must be both visually appealing and strong in content to effectively communicate the writer's messages.

5. *Where applicable, include an audit trail of document modifications.* Documents intended for *internal* use—product development support documents, those dealing with the software development life cycle, internal business plans, and so on—should include a detailed list-modification history at the beginning of the document that includes:

   - Document version number
   - Dates of changes
   - Author(s) of changes
   - Synopsis of major modifications
   - Locations of previous versions of the documents

   Additionally, a list of related documents should be included. Documents intended for *external* use, however, such as business plans documented to seek financing, should not include such an audit trail or change history. The inclusion of such material would not only have little or no importance to the readers, but might raise issues that could cloud the primary purpose of your communication.

6. *Treat each document as an original.* It is often tempting to use existing documents as baselines for an assigned document production task you might face, particularly when deadlines are tight. Because every situation is different, *each and every paragraph should be carefully reviewed* before using a "cut and paste" model of document compilation to create, for example, a business plan or a proposal.

7. *Write in a form most comfortable to you.* Even in this age of word processors and easy editing, many people—even computer professionals—are most comfortable doing an original draft in longhand and subsequently entering a document electronically. If this is the method with which you are most comfortable, don't fight it; don't feel that "if I'm a computer professional then I had better compose

at the keyboard." All writers have their own writing styles and procedures; use whatever method is most productive for you.

8. *Write and edit as needed.* First drafts are rarely the final iteration of any particular document, but excessive editing and revision can cause you to lose sight of the purpose of your writing. If successive editing passes yield little improvement in the content, you are probably getting close to the end of your editing cycle.

9. *Use tools intelligently.* Many of today's word processing packages not only include spelling checkers but also a thesaurus, grammar checking, and other capabilities. As many tools as possible should be used to increase the quality of your documents, but don't, for example, attempt to use each and every synonym for a particular word that an electronic thesaurus presents.

10. *Assume your credibility is on the line.* No matter what you write— a specifications document, a business plan, or a journal article— your professional and technical credibility is being scrutinized. Occasional mistakes are permissible; continual gross errors can damage your reputation.

Summary

In the following chapters, we'll look more closely at the different types of written communications discussed in this chapter. It is not an overstatement to note that a substantial portion of the work of the computer professional of the future will encompass written communications in the various areas above. Again, in a tightening job market within the industry, every little differentiator helps when it comes to surviving and thriving. Effective written communications (and verbal communications as well, as we will discuss in the second part of the book) can be one of those differentiators.

2

Writing
Requirements
Documents

Introduction

Nearly every version of the computer systems development life cycle model begins with the process of collecting, reviewing, and disseminating requirements for that particular information system. It is from these requirements that specifications, designs, and ultimately a completed software and/or hardware environment, are procured or developed.

It is not an overstatement to note that the documents associated with the requirements portion of the life cycle can make or break an information systems effort; while a professional, comprehensive set of documents alone may not necessarily justify a procurement or development program, poorly written or incomplete requirements documents *can and usually do* halt the process before any subsequent stages are reached.

In this chapter we will discuss the different types of requirements documents and how they relate to those in the subsequent phases of the life cycle. We'll see how requirements are distinguished from "nice to have" features, and how they should be distinguished from one another in requirements documents. We'll see how to distinguish between a "requirement" and the refinement of that requirement in a subsequent document such as one that deals with systems specifications. We'll also take a look at a sample requirements document.

What Is a "Requirement"?

It is often tempting to detail a list of requirements similar to the following, based on preconceived ideas about specific technologies, report and screen formats, and other areas:

1. An integrated UNIX-based inventory management system written on top of Oracle.
2. Input Screen 1 shall conform to illustration (. . .) below.
3. The LEDGER INTEGRATION REPORT shall contain the following columns on the second page: . . .
4. The INV_REPORT_1 module shall be integrated with the ACCTS_PAY_5 module, with the following public variables and parameters: . . .

Items such as those listed above aren't actually requirements, as considered within the context of information systems development. They *do* state a particular need, but not at the appropriate level required to provide adequate guidance and direction in development or procurement. The above statements can be considered part of the specification or design process, and have their place in one or the other of those follow-on areas.

In our context, a requirement may be viewed as a *business need,* one that must be supported by some type of information system component. If your business is running a video rental store, your requirements should be oriented toward operating that business. At a "high level" (explained later) your requirements might be:

1. Customer processing
2. Daily statistics
3. Employee processing

At a more detailed level, after refining, those requirements might be expressed as:

1. Customer processing
   a. Check out a tape
   b. Return a tape on time
   c. Return a tape late
   d. Lost tape
2. Daily statistics
   a. Number of tapes checked out
   b. Top five tapes checked out each day
   c. Number of tapes not returned on time
   d. Total revenue generated

3. Employee processing
  a. Weekly payroll
  b. Add new employee
  c. Modify employee data
  d. Delete terminated employee
  e. Employee reports
  :

Note that the above requirements make no reference to operating systems, hardware platforms, modules, interface mechanisms, screen formats, or any other implementation-specific detail. Rather, the requirements relate to the business needs necessary to successfully operate a particular type of organization.

This is not to say that requirements should be totally devoid of technical details. If, for example, you work for a computer software vendor and are creating a requirements document for a database design tool that your firm will be developing and marketing, the associated high-level requirements may be in the following form:

1. Support extended entity-relationship modeling

2. Perform normalization of design data

3. Generate SQL

In turn, these requirements might be refined as follows:

1. Support extended entity-relationship modeling
  a. Support the following design objects:
     (1) Entities
     (2) Attributes
     (3) Relationships
     (4) Hierarchies (supertypes and subtypes)
2. Perform normalization of design data
  a. Automatically generate 1st, 2nd, and 3rd normal form
  b. Generate 4th and 5th normal form at user option
3. Generate SQL
  a. Automatically generate tables, columns, and schemas
  b. Generate views with user assistance
  c. Generate DML with user assistance

In the above example, note the lack of such items as "an entity will be represented by a square," and "the tool shall run on the following operating systems: . . . . "

This is not to say that implementation-specific details such as report formats, operating system platforms, and the like aren't important to the development process; these items are, of course, absolutely necessary in order to develop or acquire the correct system for the business needs; they are covered in succeeding documents such as specifications and design documents.

A great deal of care should be given to determining if any given item is or isn't a true requirement; that is, the question should be asked, "Is this particular item a necessary one to accomplish the organization's mission, or simply a desirable one?" It is not incorrect to include items that aren't mission-critical in a requirements document; however, they should be listed under a separate heading as "desirable items" or prioritized at a lower level than the essential requirements. As discussed below, reviewers of documents should be given an understanding of the priorities of requirements relative to one another.

Requirements Documents

There are two primary categories in which requirements documents may be included: *high-level documents,* which focus on general statements of need, and *refined documents,* which take the validated requirements from the high-level documents and refine them further before the specifications process begins. High-level documents often go by such names as *Statement of Needs,* and include such items as those discussed in the preceding section. Refined documents might be referred to as a *system requirements document* or a *statement of product requirements.*

Many organizations have formal design methodologies with corresponding formal structures for these and other documents. For example, government employees or contractors who operate within the U.S. Air Force's development process develop high-level and refined requirements documents according the structure specified in the formal methodology then being used (currently the 2167-A methodology). In these types of situations, and their parallels in the corporate world, the structure of the documents you would prepare is predefined. In other situations without such a rigorous structure to which your writing must conform, you are free to develop documents in the manner you see most fit. Such documents might include the following items:

1. *Introduction and overview.* This section should describe the current information systems environment, whether manual or automated, and the purpose of issuing this requirements document (such as "Upgrade the entire corporate accounting system" or "Automate the entire chain of video stores"). Mention should be made of major shortcomings in the current mode of operation.

2. *List of requirements.* This section should contain one or more lists of the requirements, or *needs,* similar to the examples shown in the

previous section and illustrated in the sample document later in this chapter. Items that aren't essential to the mission of the organization may or may not be included, but should be designated as such by a lower priority or under a separate heading.

3. *Document review and comment procedures.* The format of comments, deadline dates, and submission criteria (to whom at what office or organization) should be stated explicitly.

The primary distinction between the format of a high-level requirements document and one oriented toward the refined list of requirements is the amount of detail among the items listed, as was demonstrated in the preceding section's examples.

If possible, requirements should be prioritized. One way is to assign a multiple-level priority distinction. (Example: Designate as 1 through 5, with priority 1 items being absolutely mandatory to continue business operations, priority 5 items being desirable but not mandatory ones, and priorities 2 through 4 on a linear scale between the two end points.) This prioritization will help give reviewers a good understanding of the needs of the information system and, for example, not cause them to reject the overall concept because they feel too many "nice to have" items are being included as real-life requirements.

Separation of Requirements Documents

In large-scale environments, requirements are often divided among several types of documents. For example, a 20,000-node, heterogeneous distributed environment that is expected to take four years to develop is an extremely complex system. To gain a better handle on your overall requirements, you might develop several types of requirements documents:

- *Overall system requirements.* This document will contain statements of overall requirements, whether they fall into the areas of hardware, software, communications, training, or some other area.

- *Software requirements.* This document will contain more detailed statements of the requirements than the "overall" document.

- *Hardware requirements.* Any requirements having to do with the hardware area might be stated in this document. While the overall philosophy of systems development promotes deferring hardware selection to latter stages of the life cycle, often there are situations where mandates exist for hardware environments. For example, there may be an organizational edict that only UNIX and MS-DOS systems that conform to certain specifications be used. If these directions are complex and lengthy, a separate document may be warranted.

- *Interface requirements.* Environments that have substantial predetermined interfaces with existing systems—both internal and external—may have those interface requirements placed into a separate document. Protocols, hardware interfaces, and other interfaces that *must* be satisfied can be placed in this type of document.

New versus Revised Systems

Depending on whether the information systems for which the requirements documents are being written is an initial development/acquisition effort, or designed to enhance or replace an existing system, the content of the listed requirements will vary somewhat. Unlike specifications documents or design documents, discussed in Chap. 3, where factors such as integration and migration are discussed in detail (example: "The new inventory system and the existing inventory system must have a dual-operation capability for a period of not less than 10 weeks, followed by a transition period not to exceed 48 hours."), requirements documents should address such issues as:

The new inventory system will supersede the existing inventory system, which has serious shortcomings in the following areas:

1. *Integration with general ledger system.* All inventory-related data must be reentered into the General Ledger system to produce consolidated journal and ledger reports.
2. *Economic order quantity (EOQ) processing.* The current inventory system does not support EOQ processing.
3. *Variances.* The current inventory system supports only cost variances, not material variance processing.

The vendor from whom the current inventory system was purchased is no longer in business, and it is impossible to upgrade the current system to meet the above requirements.

Requirements that have changed or are no longer applicable should also be noted. For example, assume that you are preparing a requirements document for version 3 of a commercial CASE tool. You might include statements such as the following:

Models. Version 3.0 will no longer support binary-relationship modeling.

Database interface. Version 3.0 will no longer retrieve metadata from commercial network databases; only relational databases will be supported.

User interface. Version 3.0 will introduce a graphical user interface (GUI) that will supplement the command line interface (CLI).

Cautions

When writing a requirements document, there is often a tendency to "go for broke" in terms of including any and all information regarding a particular systems effort. For example, you might want to include such items as the cost/benefit analysis of developing or purchasing a new system, a discussion of the technical feasibility of that system, and details about development time. As we mentioned, in most formal methodologies there are places for these other items within feasibility studies, specifications, and other documents, many of which we discuss later in this book.

It isn't wise to cloud the issues at hand by including within a requirements document material that could be handled elsewhere. Most requirements documents must undergo an approval process by corporate or organizational powers, and, especially in tough economic times when organizational funds are tight, preference is often given to the efforts whose document authors most closely follow the prevalent guidelines. Sometimes it might be beneficial to provide references to future or collateral documents that might be under way or completed (example: a feasibility study) but the bulk of those other areas shouldn't be included within a document dedicated solely to requirements.

Summary

In this chapter, we've looked at requirements documents in the context of their role as predecessors to other documents at subsequent stages of the computer system's development life cycle. Care must be taken to include the correct information in the documents. Distinctions should be made, if applicable to your organization, between high-level statements of need and derivative, more thoroughly detailed, system requirements documents.

Sample Requirements Document

Our sample requirements document is a detailed "System Requirements Document" for a national chain of video rental stores.

System Requirements Document

Zipman Video, Inc.

Video Store Management System

February 15, 1992

Prepared by:

Larry Morris
Director of Reporting

Table of Contents

Executive Summary

Current Information Systems Environment

Business Needs

Document Review Procedures

Executive Summary

In the past 12 months, Zipman, Inc. has grown from two stores to 17 units. To date, no attempts have been made to computerize operations other than the introduction of personal computers with spreadsheet functions, and this has been limited to four stores.

The Video Store Management System is necessary to achieve a number of organizational directives from management, including accurate reporting, inventory control, and employee processing.

Current Information Systems Environment

Currently, each Zipman store performs all business operations manually. Specifically:

- Customer records are maintained on a series of customer cards.
- Sales, inventory, and activity reports are collated manually from customer activity data.
- Paychecks are handwritten.
- All accounting is done manually based on various reports and payroll activity.

In addition to each store's activity, corporate headquarters performs weekly, monthly, quarterly, and annual rollups of the aggregate information from each store. All corporate headquarters activities are performed manually.

The only automation is sporadic use of spreadsheets in four stores. Each of these stores has attempted, with limited success, to maintain logs of activity information in spreadsheet form. Each store has customized its own templates for its own use, and no integration of this information is possible. Each spreadsheet program is an old (circa 1983) version with no multiple sheet links.

Business Needs

Listed below is the consolidated list of requirements for the proposed Video Store Management System. Priorities of all requirements are listed, using a scale of:

1. Highest priority—essential for continued business operations
2. High priority—essential for business productivity
3. Average priority—would greatly aid business productivity

Each area listed below includes a number of items that are required of that area. Each of these items would have a corresponding functional instantiation in the Video Store Management System.

Area 1: Customer processing

Item	Priority
Customer checks out a tape	1
Customer returns a tape on time	1
Customer returns a tape late	1
Customer loses or damages a tape	1
Access customer information from another store	2
Get customer activity for contests	3
Mailing list of customers for promotions	3

Area 2: Daily statistics

Item	Priority
Provide number of tapes checked out for day	2
List top five tapes checked out each day	3
Provide number of tapes out with customers	2
Provide number of tapes out that are late	2
List total revenue by tape category	2
List total revenue	1

Each of the above statistics and reports must be done on a by-store basis as well as for the aggregate of all stores.

Area 3: Periodic statistics

Item	Priority
Provide number of tapes checked during period	2
List top five tapes checked during period	3
List number of times each tape was checked out during period	2
Provide total number of tapes out that were returned late	2
List top five tapes returned late	2
List total revenue by tape category during period	2
List total revenue during period	1
Provide comparative reports for any of the above; stores can be compared against one another, and the period can be compared against the corresponding period in the past year, two years, or three years.	2

Each of the above statistics and reports must be done on a by-store basis as well as for the aggregate of all stores. Each statistic and report is needed on a weekly, monthly, quarterly, or annual basis. Historical data must be retrievable.

Area 4: Employee processing

Item	Priority
Add a new employee	1
Modify an employee's record (personal data, payroll)	1
Delete an employee	1
Process payroll	1
Schedule employees into stores for the upcoming week	1
Get tax information for federal and state agencies	1
Issue W-2s	2

Area 5: Inventory management

Item	Priority
Put new tapes into inventory	2
Produce list of all tapes and counts for each	1
Delete tapes from inventory	2
Adjust inventory based on physical count	1
Automatically order new releases	2

Document Review Procedures

Please review this document and address all comments, corrections, and other responses by March 3, 1992, to:

Larry Morris
Director of Reporting
Speedway Headquarters
2222 Speedway Blvd.
(602) 555-0000

3

Writing Specifications and Design Documents

Introduction

In most situations, the logical successor to the requirements documents discussed in Chap. 2 is a system specifications document, which in turn is usually followed by one or more design documents. In this chapter we'll take a look at the contents of these respective documents.

Specifications

As we discussed in the preceding chapter, the primary purpose of requirements documents—both high-level and detailed—is to gather a consolidated list of business needs, prioritize them, and provide a central reference point to which all persons involved can provide feedback.

Following the validation of these requirements, it is the responsibility of those involved in the development life cycle to translate each requirement into one or more specification items. As with requirements, a definition of "specification" is in order to place the process in context.

A specification can be viewed as a *general* statement of what must be accomplished in an information system. Caution should be taken to ensure that prospective solutions, whether generic or implementation-specific, not influence the form of the specification statement. For example:

Employee processing should utilize a client/server architecture, using an object-oriented database as the data storage layer.

The statement above is likely to be far too restrictive to be of much value in a specifications document. Rather, it is oriented more to the design stage and corresponding documents for that process; these are discussed later in this chapter.

One way to look at specifications is to see them in the context of requirements. For example, in the preceding chapter we saw the following requirement:

Area 1: Customer processing

Item	Priority
Customer checks out a tape	1

This requirement might be refined into a specification as follows:

1. *Customer checks out a tape.* When a customer checks out one or more tapes, his or her customer file is accessed and checked for positive and negative items. Negative items include overdue tapes and outstanding payments owed. Positive items include membership in the *Frequent Renter* program. This transaction history must be checked against activity at all stores. Any current in-store specials or customer discounts are applied to the amount due. Following payment for the rental, the customer's file is updated with the tape or tapes checked out and the due dates.

The specification lists each component and item that must be accomplished to meet the requirement it represents. Note that no mention is made of the sequence in which the processing is executed, the programming language in which code might be written, underlying databases or table formats, program flow control, or any other issue that deals with the *implementation* of that specification. Rather, the specification concentrates on stating *what* must be done, not *how* it will be accomplished.

As with requirements documents, this does not mean that specifications must not be devoid of technical details. As with the requirement from which it comes, a product specification produced by a vendor for a commercial software package will feature an appropriate level of technical information about supported hardware and operating system platforms, product features, and other items.

Relationship to RFPs

In Chap. 6 we discuss writing requests for proposals (RFPs). An RFP is the appropriate vehicle to take the items presented in a specifications document and "announce them to the world" in order to solicit proposed solutions in the form of proposals (Chap. 7). That is, an approved list of specified items and features can then, with appropriate enhancements, form the basis of an RFP document.

When discussing RFPs, we stress the importance of language selection to ensure that respondents can distinguish between optional and mandatory system features. Since specifications documents are intended for internal use, discussion, and modification, the selection of language (such as ensuring that "shall" is used instead of "may," for example) is not necessarily as critical as in RFPs, where the document may become part of the contractual process. Care should still be taken when writing a specifications document to be sure that distinctions between mandatory and optional portions of the system are identified clearly.

Design Documents

The "classical model" for design documents, and the design process in general, should include three levels, with ever-increasing amounts in detail:

1. *Conceptual.* The highest-level, most abstract form of design; a conceptual design still has plenty of room for implementation-specific details.
2. *Logical.* A more refined level of design; a logical design includes decisions made as to specific protocols, platforms (example: What database management system will be the underlying layer?"), and other mechanisms.
3. *Physical, or implementation-specific.* This level is the closest to actual coding and development. Decisions such as implementation language and others must be made by this point, if not sooner.

Figure 3.1 illustrates the three levels of design with respect to the amounts of abstraction and detail included.

Following this classical model of design levels, a corresponding number of design document levels usually is used. That is, a specification will be refined into a conceptual design, which is further refined into a logical design, which in turn is finalized into an implementation-specific design. In reality, though, these design levels are often compressed into two, or even one, continual design process as deadlines, resource problems, and other real-world issues come into play during the development process.

In any case, there should still be a clear understanding of the proper contents of each type of design document. When asked to prepare a de-

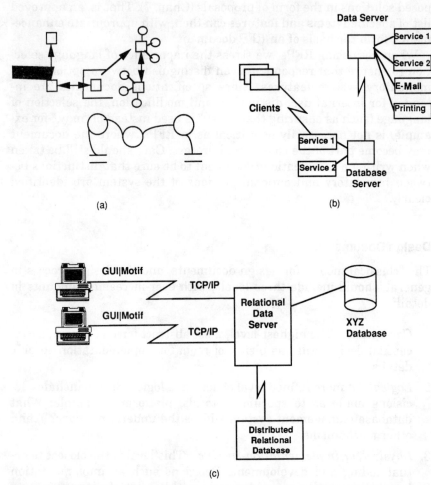

Figure 3.1 Three levels of design: (*a*) conceptual; (*b*) logical; (*c*) physical, or implementation-specific.

sign document, your actions and resulting work will vary according to the input with which you are able to work. If, for example, you are given a specification and told to produce a design document, you should begin at the conceptual design process, and your initial effort should be concentrated around conceptual issues such as abstract connections, entity-relationship models, and other conceptual tools. Even if your assigned target is an implementation-specific design to be used by developers, *failure to include the conceptual design process and the corresponding documentation can be detrimental to the development process.*

Similarly, if you are given a logical design with which to work, you should target your design documents toward physical design rather than conceptual work, since you can assume that the conceptual design has been completed and validated. The logical sequence of the steps should be preserved in your efforts.

Design documents are the point at which you switch your orientation from "what must be done" to "how it will be done." Correspondingly, design documents should be heavily oriented toward graphical contents. Inclusion of entity-relationship database designs, data flow diagrams, structure charts, context diagrams, and other graphical tools can help tell others *how* a particular process will be accomplished when actual development begins.

Other tools, such as pseudocode (English-like instructions without having to worry about programming language syntax) are also valuable in the lower-level, implementation-specific design documents.

Summary

The most important thing to remember about the material covered in this chapter is that as situations vary, so do the contents of specifications and various types of design documents. As long as you keep in mind the basic principles of each area with respect to degree of detail and appropriate levels of abstraction, you can adjust your writing to any situation, based on the amount and kind of documents that must be produced. Even when two or more of these documents are compressed into one, the basic tenets still apply as designated by each area of the system life cycle to which the documents are oriented.

Sample Specifications Document

Our sample specifications document is the follow-on to the sample requirements document in Chap. 2. In our example, the system requirements for Zipman Video have been validated, and approval has been granted to prepare a systems specification for the Video Store Management System.

System Specifications

Zipman Video, Inc.

Video Store Management System

April 21, 1992

Prepared by:

Larry Morris
Director of Reporting

Table of Contents

Executive Summary

System Specifications

Document Review Procedures

Executive Summary

Zipman, Inc. is preparing to issue a Request for Proposals (RFP) to system developers and consultants, the purpose of which is to acquire a Video Store Management System (VSMS). The items presented in this specifications document have been derived from the approved System Requirements Document of February 15, 1992.

Following validation and approval of these items, the RFP will be issued (estimated issuance date: June 30, 1992) with an expected response time of 45 days.

The comment and review procedures for this specification are provided at the end of this document.

Systems Specifications

Area 1: Customer processing

This primary functional area contains all processing related to Zipman customers. The bulk of the functional items deal with customer rentals and returns, though additional features are included that deal with store promotions. The customer processing area shall support the following business functions:

1. *Customer checks out a tape.* When a customer checks out one or more tapes, his or her customer file is accessed and checked for positive and negative items. Negative items include overdue tapes and outstanding payments owed. Positive items include membership in the *Frequent Renter* program. This transaction history must be checked against activity at all Zipman stores. Any current in-store specials or customer discounts are applied to the amount due. Following payment for the rental, the customer's file is updated with the tape or tapes checked out and the due dates.

2. *Customer returns a tape.* When a customer returns one or more tapes, his or her file must be accessed to determine if the returns are being made on time or late. If the returns are on time, no additional charges are assessed, and the customer's outstanding tape list is cleared. If the returns are late, the appropriate late charge (as specified in each store's policy) is assessed, and the money is collected from the customer. The customer's file must be notated with the late return. The tapes are then checked back into inventory. Any returns to a Zipman store other than the one at which the tape or tapes was/were rented must access any remote customer information and remote inventory information.

3. *Customer loses or damages a tape.* If a customer returns a tape that is damaged, or reports that a tape has been lost, the appropriate penalty fees (as designated by each store) are assessed against the customer. The customer's file is notated with the loss or damage. The tape must then be removed from current inventory.

4. *Access customer information from another store.* Any Zipman customer can check out any tape from any store, or return a tape checked out at one store to another.

5. *Get customer activity for contests.* Searches of customer files can be made to determine those customers who have rented the most

tapes during a given period to time, or those who have rented some or all of a certain series of tapes (example: all *Star Trek* movie plus series show tapes) during a given period of time. This information is used for contests.

6. *Mailing list of customers for promotions.* Any store operator or corporate headquarters staff person will be able to print mailing labels of all customers of the entire chain or for one or more individual stores. These are for mailing lists.

7. *Correct customer file.* Authorized employees (those with appropriate permissions) can access and update a customer file to remove incorrect information or change the stored information, based on store and corporate policies. A log of all corrections must be maintained.

Area 2: Daily statistics

Each of the statistics listed below must be able to be run at an individual Zipman store, based on the day's activity at that store, and at corporate headquarters, with the operator being able to specify any combination of stores to include an individual store, any two, any three, . . . or all stores. However, no store manager at an individual store can run statistics reports for a store other than his or her own.

1. *Provide tape activity for the day.* This report will give the number of VHS and Beta tapes checked out during the day, as well as VHS and Beta tapes checked back in. It will also flag the tapes that were checked in and went back out the same day.

2. *List top five tapes checked out each day.* This report will give the five titles with the most copies checked out for the day. For aggregate reports run from corporate headquarters, this report will give the corporate-wide total, as well as the top five titles at each store included in the report.

3. *Provide number of tapes out with customers.* This report will give the total number of tapes that are currently out of inventory, including all that are still within deadline and all that are late. For those that aren't late, it will provide a breakdown between one- and two-day rentals.

4. *Provide number of tapes out that are late.* This report will be a subset of the one above, except that it will provide information only about the number of tapes that are overdue (along with a list of customers who have those tapes).

5. *List total revenue by tape category.* This report will provide the total revenue for the day according to the following categories:

- Comedy
- Adventure
- Horror
- Romance
- Children's
- Sports
- Documentary
- Other

6. *List total revenue.* This report will provide the total revenue for all tapes checked out for the day.

Area 3: Periodic statistics

These statistics will be nearly identical to those listed above, except that the operator can specify any period in the list below from which to calculate the statistics:

1. Current week to date
2. Last completed week
3. Current month to date
4. Last completed month
5. Current quarter to date
6. Last completed quarter
7. Current year to date
8. Other (specify beginning and ending dates for the statistics)

Additionally, comparative statistics can be specified as follows:

1. Any store can be compared against another.
2. Any period from the above list (Nos. 1–8) can be compared against the equivalent period from the previous year. [Example: "Current quarter to date" (No. 5) will be compared against the same number of business days in last year's equivalent period.]

The statistics include:

1. *Provide tape activity during the period.* This report will give the number of VHS and Beta tapes checked out during the period, as well as VHS and Beta tapes checked back in.

2. *List top five tapes checked out during the period.* This report will give the five titles with the most copies checked out during the period. For aggregate reports run from corporate headquarters, this report will give the corporate-wide total, as well as the top five titles at each store included in the report.

3. *Provide average number of tapes out with customers.* This report will give the average number of tapes that were out of inventory at the close of each business day.

4. *Provide total number of tapes returned late, returned damaged, or lost.* This report will be a subset of the one above, except will provide information only about the number of tapes that were returned overdue, the number that were returned damaged, and the number of tapes lost during the period.

5. *List total revenue by tape category.* This report will provide the total revenue for the period according to the following categories:

   - Comedy
   - Adventure
   - Horror
   - Romance
   - Children's
   - Sports
   - Documentary
   - Other

6. *List total revenue.* This report will provide the total revenue for all tapes checked out during the period.

Area 4: Employee processing

This area will contain all functions dealing with employees and payroll. Only store managers or authorized corporate headquarters personnel can access functions in this area, and store managers can access only the information for their respective employees. These functions include:

1. *Add a new employee.* When an employee is hired, the following information is collected about him or her and added to the employee's file:

Name
Address
Telephone
Work history
Current salary or hourly wages
Bonus status
Work status (full-time, part-time)
Tax information (number of withholdings, marital status for filing purposes)

2. *Modify an employee's record.* Any of the above information can be modified upon change.

3. *Delete an employee.* When an employee terminates, his or her information is deleted from the active employee roster and archived in the past employee log. Reason for termination is added to the archived information.

4. *Process payroll.* Each week, payroll is processed from time card information and salary/hourly wage information. Checks are issued.

5. *Schedule employees into stores for the upcoming week.* Each store can access its list of employees, plus those from other stores allocated to the "schedule pool," and prepare the draft upcoming week's schedule. Each employee's schedule is added to his or her current record.

6. *Get tax information for federal and state agencies.* When tax reporting periods occur, salary and withholding information is gathered from employees' files and submitted to the appropriate agency.

7. *Issue W-2s.* W-2 documents are issued based on salary and withholding information contained in the employees' files.

Area 5: Inventory management

This area contains all functions relating to inventory management. Some of these functions are cross-related to those of Area 1, customer processing, since most customer activities cause tapes to be temporarily removed from inventory or added back into inventory. Inventory reports can be performed on an individual store basis or for any or all stores. Managers *can* access inventory information from another store. The functions of this area include:

1. *Put new tapes into inventory.* When new tapes arrive at a store, the order list is checked to ensure that all tapes ordered have been received. Discrepancies are noted. The inventory count for that store is then updated.

2. *Produce list of all tapes and counts for each.* A list of all titles, broken down by VHS and Beta, can be produced, with the numbers of each title at the store or stores included in the report list.

3. *Delete tapes from inventory.* Lost, damaged, or tapes no longer used can be deleted from the inventory.

4. *Adjust inventory based on physical count.* Following periodic physical counts, the computerized inventory can be updated based on the results.

5. *Transfer inventory from one store to another.* Requests to transfer a tape from one store to another, or returns to a store of a tape checked out elsewhere, shall enact the transfer of the item or items from one store's inventory to another.

6. *Automatically order new releases.* New releases can be ordered automatically based on the integration with the XYZ Tape Distributor automatic ordering system. New releases on order shall be flagged at each store and a report can be produced showing what has been ordered and when it is due.

Document Review Procedures

Please review this document and address all comments, corrections, and other responses by May 30, 1992 to:

Larry Morris
Director of Reporting
Speedway Headquarters
2222 Speedway Blvd.
(602) 555-0000

Sample Conceptual Design Document

Our sample conceptual design document is also related to Chap. 2's sample requirements document. In our example, the system specifications from the preceding document have been approved, and high-level conceptual design has commenced internally rather than externally. In the interest of saving space, we will present primarily the graphical aspects of the conceptual design document, along with some of the narrative; a full-scale design document will be—like the other documents—lengthier and more complex.

Conceptual Data and Procedural Design

Zipman Video, Inc.

Video Store Management System

June 21, 1992

Prepared by:

Larry Morris,
Director of Reporting

Table of Contents

Introduction

Top-Level Data Flow Diagram

Customer Processing, Level 1

Daily Statistics, Level 1

Periodic Statistics, Level 1

Employee Processing, Level 1

Inventory Management, Level 1

Entity-Relationship Diagram

Attribute Properties

Introduction

This document contains the conceptual design for the Zipman Video system. The graphical designs contained in this document are derived from the approved System Specifications document of April 21, 1992.

The designs of this document will be reviewed at a design walkthrough currently scheduled for July 15, 1992.

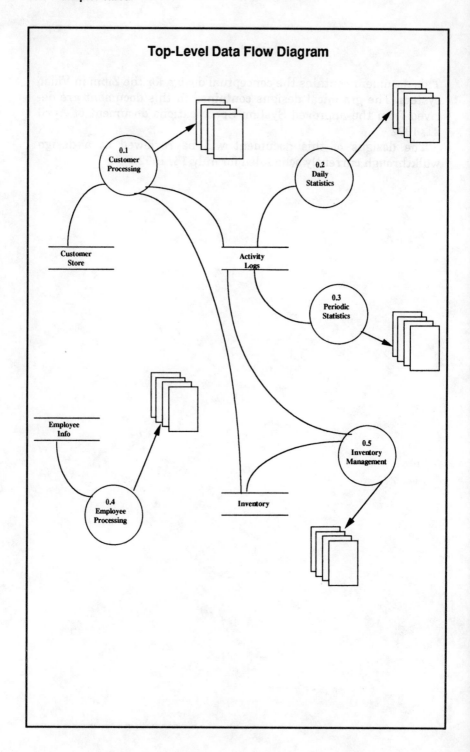

Top-Level Data Flow Diagram

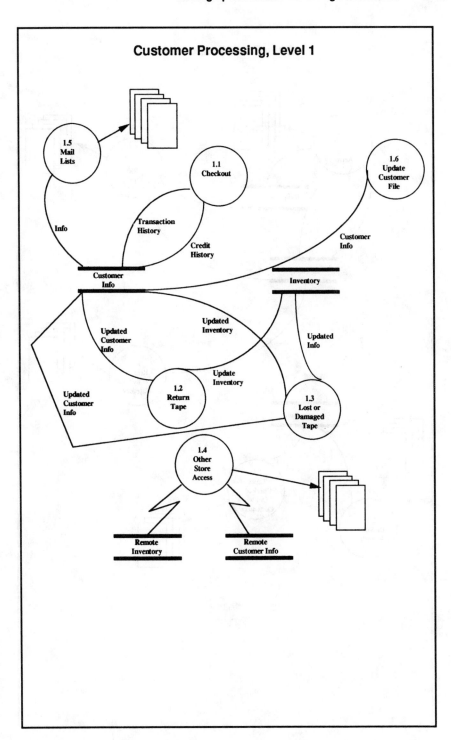

Customer Processing, Level 1

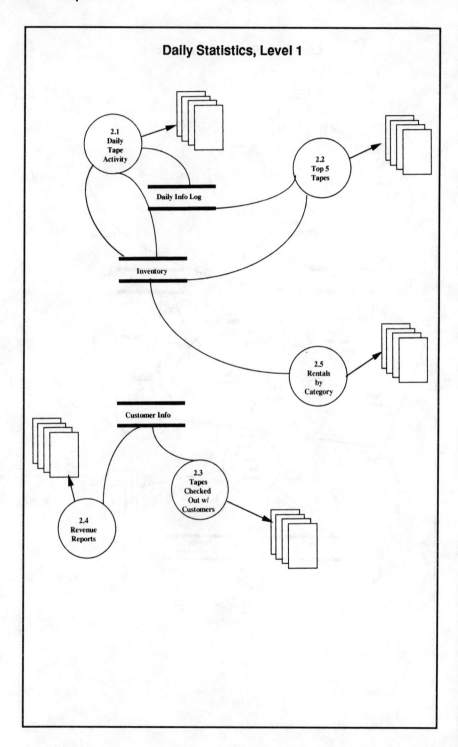

Daily Statistics, Level 1

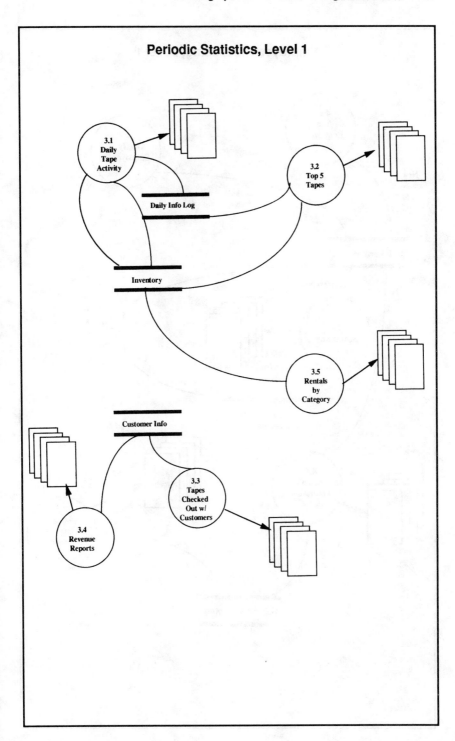

Periodic Statistics, Level 1

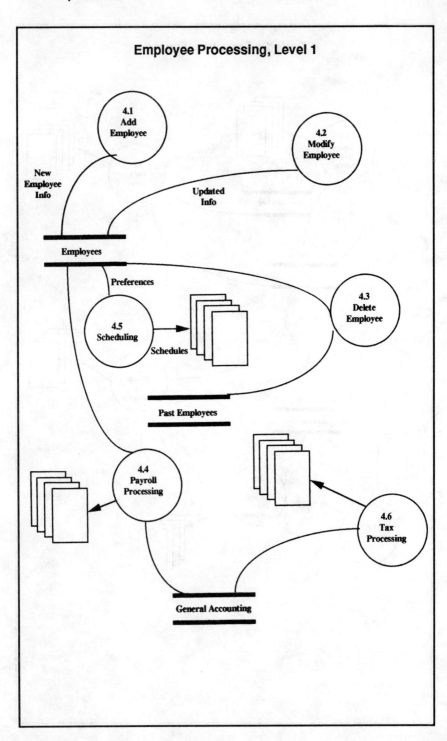

Employee Processing, Level 1

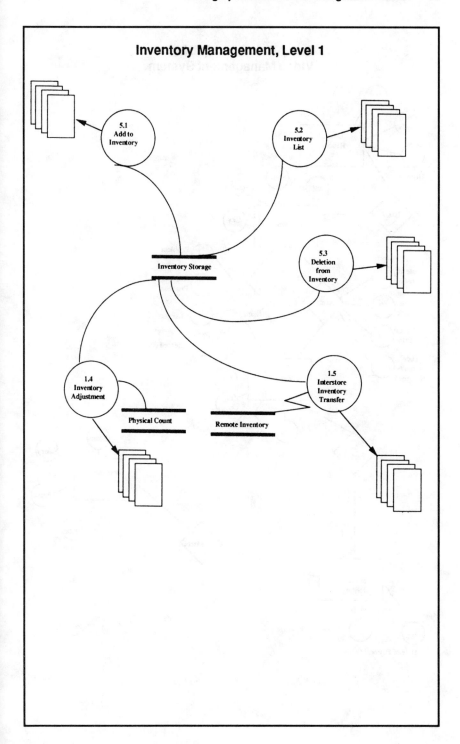

Inventory Management, Level 1

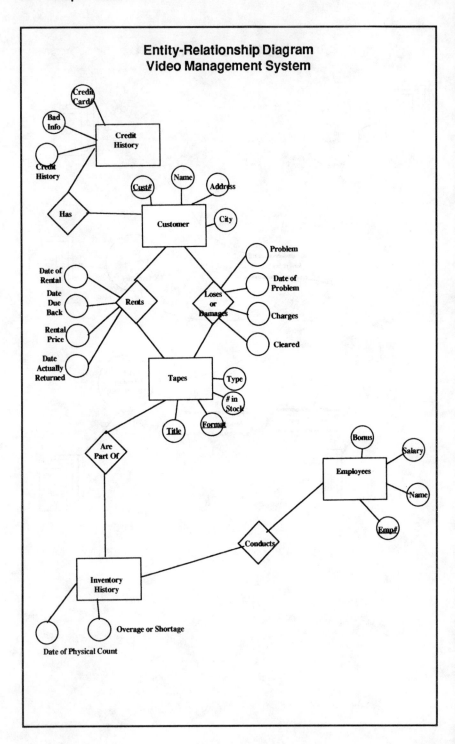

Entity-Relationship Diagram
Video Management System

Attribute Properties

Employees

Emp# -
  numeric integer
  6 digits
  not null
  primary key

Name -
  variable character
  50 spaces
  not null
  candidate key, but
    not unique

Salary -
  decimal
  8 digits, plus 2 decimal places
  not null
  range check: greater than
    $10,000, less than $200,000
  not unique

Bonus
  decimal
  8 digits, plus 2 decimal places
  not null
  range check: less than $30,000
  not unique

Tapes

Title -
  variable character
  50 spaces
  not null
  part of primary key

Format -
  variable character
  10 spaces
  not null
  part of primary key
  list of values check:
    VHS, Beta, Laser Disk

 # in stock -
  integer
  3 digits
  not null
  range check: positive number

Type -
  variable character
  15 spaces
  list of values check: Children's,
    Horror, Comedy, Romance,
    Other

Attribute Properties

Customer

Cust # -
  numeric integer
  6 digits
  not null
  primary key

Name -
  variable character
  50 spaces
  not null
  candidate key, but
    not unique

Address -
  variable character
  50 spaces

City -
  variable character
  20 spaces

Inventory History

Date of physical count -
  date
  range of values check: between
    1/1/80 and 12/31/2100

Overage or shortage -
  integer
  4 digits

Credit History

Credit card # -
  integer
  20 digits
  not null

Bad info -
  character
  3 digits
  must be 'Yes' or 'No'

Credit history -
  data type TBD
  may be repeating group

Attribute Properties

Note: Relationship attributes will likely be transformed into
entity attributes during logical design stage.

Rents (relationship)

Date of rental -
  date
  range of values: between 1/1/80 and 12/31/2100
  not null

Date due back -
  date
  range of values: between 1/1/80 and 12/31/2100
  not null

Rental price -
  decimal
  2 digits, plus 2 decimal places
  not null
  range of values: positive number, less than $100.00

Date actually returned -
  date
  range of values: between 1/1/80 and 12/31/2100
  not null

Loses or damages (relationship)

Problem -
  variable character
  100 spaces
  not null

Date of Problem -
  date
  range of values: between 1/1/80 and 12/31/2100
  not null

Charges -
  decimal
  3 digits, plus 2 decimal places
  range of values: positive number

Cleared -
  Boolean

4

Feasibility Studies

A business plan, as we will discuss in Chap. 8, enables you to analyze a new concept from many business angles, including finance and marketing, so that you can communicate your intentions to your reader. As a computer professional you may be faced with various circumstances in which you are required to determine the course of action for a computer concept, whether for new software development or for a client, to determine the most appropriate systems installation. The first step, however, involves your analysis of the concept's feasibility. This entails a feasibility study.

Feasibility Study Components

Feasibility studies are a form of written communication. While these studies may not fit neatly into the definition of written communication, nonetheless they provide you with a communication device that is your business plan in an embryonic state. Feasibility studies vary in terms of their length and the issues they analyze. While there are no hard and fast rules as to what to include in the typical study, there are basic components that should at least be examined in all feasibility studies.

1. *Concept.* This is the crux of your feasibility study—the reason for the feasibility study in the first place. This component of the study enables you to write down, usually for the first time in an organized manner, the concept you want to achieve. Once you can write and communicate what the concept is to be, you have the foundation to determine if your concept is "doable," or as you ask in a feasibility study, is it feasible?

The following components of a feasibility study require you to wear three very distinct hats. Each of these feasibility components requires you to delve deeply into the respective area to perform a proper analysis. However, it is important to keep in mind at all times that these analyses, by default, are interrelated and to a large extent dependent on one another's outcome for the final answer to your feasibility question. Accordingly, this interrelationship should be in the back of your mind throughout the individual analyses you perform. We will examine this interrelationship after we have discussed these components.

2. *Market feasibility.* Once you have definitively defined your concept, your next task is to determine if a market exists. Your business plan will thoroughly examine the marketing of your concept; your task here is to determine whether a market exists which will provide an outlet for the exchange of compensation. In other words, this portion of your study will determine if your concept is a marketable entity.

3. *Technical feasibility.* No matter how unique or dynamic the concept, you must determine if it is technically feasible. While at first glance this may seem obvious, it is often overlooked in the excitement of a new and innovative concept. If your feasibility study involves the integration into an existing system, does the technology exist or can you develop what you need within the required time frame? As we will discuss in Chap. 8, Developing Business Plans, a definitive time table is part of your overall business plan. Thus, your time table implicitly has an underlying technological link: Can you technologically achieve what you need in the designated time frame? The answer to this question is a component of the overall answer to your feasibility study.

4. *Financial feasibility.* At this point in your feasibility study, you have analyzed the market and the technology as they relate to your concept. As may be expected, economics comes into the picture at this point. The financial feasibility portion of your study determines if the concept is viable in financial terms. The numbers required to perform an accurate financial feasibility study may not yet be available. In such a case this analysis requires you to make a variety of assumptions; it is often beneficial to perform worst and best case financial feasibility studies to view the possible ranges of financial outcomes.

The interrelationship of the aforementioned feasibility components is best highlighted by way of example. If a company is looking to upgrade its computer system, what it wants may be financially feasible but not technically feasible, or vice versa. This illustration is designed to show that feasibility studies are similar to business plans and requests for proposals in that they are all situationally dependent; they may be financially or technically slanted. Regardless of this slant, there is a strong interaction between these two components in a feasibility study.

In our previous example, the lower cost alternative might not be technically feasible.

When commercial software is available, does it fit into your time frame? If it is not available, can you develop it? If you can develop the software, is it financially feasible? This series of questions illustrates the interrelationship of the various feasibility components of your study.

There is one additional feasibility component you should analyze in your study. Throughout this book, we attempt to have you view various business practices, such as business plans and requests for proposals, as communication tools. As a communication device, feasibility studies also require you to perform your own self-evaluation to determine if you have the ability to proceed. No matter what the computer orientation, you need to feel confident that you have the ability and determination to proceed with your concept. This personal feasibility is a component that should be examined in every feasibility study.

Uses for Feasibility Studies

Feasibility studies are appropriate and even necessary in a variety of situations. Remember, this study is intended to lay the foundation for the analysis that will determine whether your concept can become a viable, working product or service.

The following are situations which warrant a feasibility study. As previously mentioned, however, you must be aware that different facets of the feasibility study will require varying degrees of emphasis.

1. *Buying a new system.* The feasibility study performed under this scenario will enable you to determine if the system you intend to recommend is both financially and technically feasible.

2. *Converting from old system to new system.* The conversion of systems necessitates a feasibility study to discover if integration of the existing software, if warranted, is possible. This study will emphasize the technological aspect of the feasibility study.

3. *In-house project vs. outside contracting.* Many computer professionals will find themselves in a business situation that requires them to determine who is best suited to accomplish the task at hand. The feasibility study will enable you to compare the most appropriate course of action from a financial viewpoint, while simultaneously providing you with insight into the technological advantages and disadvantages of each option.

4. *Deciding among development projects.* The economic environment of limited capital, more prevalent today than at any time in recent memory, may require you to choose among various projects to deter-

mine which is the most feasible. The feasibility study will enable you to answer this question and prevent you from wasting valuable time and limited capital on projects that are sound in concept but not feasible in reality.

Summary

Feasibility studies are designed to help you decide whether your concept is practical. They enable you to view your concept from financial, marketing, and technology vantage points. The resulting micro feasibility analyses collectively enable you to form a macro analysis to answer the overall question of feasibility.

An important word of caution: objectivity. Your objectivity is crucial to your credibility. Your bias could taint your objectivity, resulting in faulty assumptions. Accordingly, it is important to be objective and impartial throughout the feasibility study.

Sample Feasibility Study

The feasibility study that follows provides you with an example of the financial component of a feasibility study. In our example, Edna Meza, a computer consultant, has been retained by the William H. Kelley Corporation to determine the feasibility of a conversion to a new computer system. Debra Queen, vice president of the William H. Kelley Corporation, has asked Meza to present her with a financial feasibility analysis on this conversion.

You will note that this financial feasibility study includes financial data using the concept of present value [discussed in Chap. 6, Writing Requests for Proposals (RFPs)]. If your analysis includes multiple years for financial comparison, it is important to include present value as part of your financial feasibility analysis; you will note the difference between total dollar savings and present value savings in Table 2.

TABLE 1   Five-Year Ownership Cost of Existing System with Upgrade;
Financial Feasibility Analysis
William H. Kelley Corporation, Option 1

Year	1	2	3	4	5
Hardware:					
Upgrades/purchases			45,000	51,600	
Hardware maintenance	136,000	136,000	137,500	138,000	139,800
Subtotal hardware	136,000	136,000	182,500	189,600	139,800
Software:					
Upgrades/purchases	8,000	12,300	14,800	16,300	
Software maintenance and licenses	104,600	108,000	108,000	110,500	112,000
Subtotal software	112,600	120,300	122,800	126,800	112,000
Staffing		26,000		36,700	
Annual expenses	248,600	282,300	305,300	353,100	251,800
Total expenditures		$1,441,100			

TABLE 2   Five-Year Ownership Cost of New System;
Financial Feasibility Analysis
William H. Kelley Corporation, Option 2

Year	1	2	3	4	5
Hardware:					
Maintenance of current system, 2 years	136,000	136,000			
New system:					
Purchases	75,000	60,000			35,000
Hardware maintenance	11,000	12,000	15,300	18,000	18,400
Subtotal hardware	222,000	208,000	15,300	18,000	53,400
Software:					
Maintenance of current system, 2 years					
Software maintenance and licenses	104,600	108,000			
New system:					
Purchases/development	88,000	27,800		17,500	
Software maintenance	13,600	15,300	15,300	18,500	6,100
Subtotal software	206,200	151,100	15,300	36,000	6,100
Staffing/outside consulting	185,000	185,000			
Annual expenses	613,200	544,100	30,600	54,000	59,500

Total expenditures	$1,301,400
Net present value of expenditures @ 8%	$1,138,733
Savings from conversion over five-year period:	
Total dollar savings	$ 139,700
Present value savings	$ 6,745

5

Documentation

Introduction

Of all the types of writing we discuss in this book, the one most likely to be left to "professionals" to develop is documentation. Large companies and organizations, primarily vendors but also user-oriented organizations, usually have a staff of technical writers who specialize in writing the various types of documentation we will discuss in this chapter. The traditional model is that programmers, analysts, engineers, and others develop the hardware and software, while technical writers produce the accompanying documentation.

There are many cases, however, where the average computer professional must be responsible for preparing various types of documentation. Many smaller companies do not have a staff of technical writers, so the documentation of how to use software and hardware is left to the same people who produce the products. Many computer professionals have small consulting and contract development firms, and find themselves responsible for documenting their work to their clients. Even in large organizations where commercial products—each with its accompanying documentation—are integrated with one another, a responsibility still exists to provide users with guidance to such items as customized menus and error recovery procedures.

In this chapter, we'll discuss the different types of documentation and how they differ from each other in form and intended audience. We'll look at suggested components of these types of documentation, and discuss some guidelines to consider when preparing documentation.

Trends in Documentation

Before we discuss some of the categories into which documentation can be classified, it would be beneficial to discuss some of the trends that affect how documentation is developed: reduced size, on-line documentation, and limited cross-documentation.

Size.   The introduction of the Apple Macintosh in 1984 began a number of trends in personal computing, primarily in the use of *graphical user interfaces* (GUIs). Another trend, which was somewhat less noticeable, was the reduced size of the documentation that accompanied hardware and software products. Traditionally, computer products had been accompanied by voluminous documentation, which was often divided into multiple volumes. Much of the original documentation from Apple computer and from third-party developers with Macintosh-based products was praised for its brevity and conciseness. The trend has carried over to other computer systems as well.

It would be self-defeating to advertise hardware and software with the main marketing message of "easy to use" and still need to provide hundreds of pages of documentation for users, both casual and experienced. The self-explanatory nature of today's graphics-based software has done a great deal to reduce the need for as much documentation as in the past. Similarly, the graphical orientation helps instantiate the "picture is worth a thousand words" philosophy; the ability to show a sample screen with several menu bars or dialog boxes results in less space being needed than the corresponding verbiage would have made necessary to describe a command line interface step by step.

As we will discuss later, there are still instances, such as programming reference manuals, where comprehensive, voluminous documentation is still required. For user-oriented documentation, however, the trend has been toward smaller documentation sets, and this trend is likely to continue.

On-line documentation.   The growth of hypertext facilities and other software searching techniques has led to an increase in on-line documentation. Software has long featured interactive help facilities and textual copies of documentation that could be retrieved. In most cases, the retrieval mechanisms were awkward and unable to be used in traditional single-tasking personal computer environments; the software in question had to be exited by the user and the documentation accessed through a text editor or word processor, a process that usually took longer than grabbing the manual from the shelf.

The linked retrieval aspects of hypertext, coupled with multitasking and windowed environments, has led to strong growth in on-line documentation and manuals. Features such as context-sensitive help, where a particular feature can be highlighted and the appropriate documentation accessed via a menu choice or on-screen "button," have helped accelerate this trend.

It is unlikely that in the near future on-line documentation will fully replace written manuals. Many computer users still interact through single-function personal computers or character cell "dumb" terminals, and don't have the prerequisite user environments necessary to facilitate use of on-line documentation. All documentation, however, should be created with the needs of both on-line and book-form use in mind.

Limited cross-documentation. A subset of the size reduction trend we discussed earlier is the reduction in cross-documentation; that is, the number of times in a documentation set that a particular feature or command is referenced. Assume, as an example, that a particular software product XYZ has a documentation set that consists of the following manuals:

- XYZ Installation Guide
- Getting Started with XYZ
- XYZ User's Manual
- XYZ Programming Manual
- XYZ Reference Manual

In traditional models, you might find a section entitled "Starting XYZ from DOS" in each of the manuals. Likewise, you might also find sections dealing with "Creating an XYZ Document" in most or all manuals. These duplicate references have been a primary cause of the excessive size of most documentation sets.

As we will discuss, there is often still a need for separate manuals, or at least separate sections within the same manual, called the *User's Guide* and the *Comprehensive Reference Manual*. In many cases, however, the detailed explanation of "Starting" or "Creating a Document" are relegated to one place, with other portions having cross-references to that place rather than repetitive documentation.

Note also that the trend in on-line documentation, with its hypertext base, effectively eliminates this problem. A single instance of a particular feature or command may be present in the on-line documentation, with multiple pointers or links along, for example, the "user's guide" and "reference" paths.

Types of Documentation

Let's take a more detailed look at some of the different types of documentation you might be called upon to produce. Keep in mind that we refer to each of the types below as a *guide* or *manual*. In reality, a single volume might contain several or all of the types discussed below if the total number of pages can easily fit into a single document. In such a case, a single *product documentation* volume might have individual sections for "Installation," "Getting Started," "User's Guide," and "Reference." In many cases, however, these different types are still produced as separate manuals.

User's guides

User's guides traditionally are oriented toward the logical order in which an operator will use a computer product. For example, a user's guide for a word processing package called MightyWord might be organized as follows:

Chapter 1 Starting MightyWord

Chapter 2 Basic Operations

Creating Text
Saving and Recalling Files
Text Attributes
Setting Margins

Chapter 3 Printing with MightyWord

Selecting Default Printers
Printing an Entire Document
Printing Portions of a Document
Spooled Printing

Chapter 4 Advanced Features

Editing Files from Other Word Processors
Setting Multiple Margins
Inserting Graphics into Text

Note that the organization of the contents is oriented around *how* a typical user might use the product. No effort is made to provide, for example, alphabetical lists of commands, as would be appropriate for a comprehensive reference manual (discussed later). Also, individual subjects (example: basic margin operations and advanced margin operations) may be split among different sections within the guide. User's guides are often organized into two distinct parts:

1. A "quick start" user's guide, oriented towards experienced users (such as users of a previous version of the product). Wording in a *quick start* portion is often more terse, less verbose, and oriented to-

ward an attitude of "To do ABC, press DEF and figure out the rest." The *quick start* portion is not intended to be as comprehensive as a user's guide, but rather to provide the experienced user with a consolidated, short reference to the critical items he or she needs to know to begin exploratory operations of the product.

2. The "regular" user's guide, as discussed above.

Reference manuals

Unlike a user's guide, a reference manual is intended to serve as a single, authoritative source of a product's or system's operations. Entries often are organized alphabetically or functionally (by menu bar item, for example). Usually, no effort is made to distinguish between "basic" and "advanced" operations; all operations are treated equally.

For example, the sample MightyWord Reference Manual that would accompany the user's guide illustrated above might appear as follows:

Chapter 1 Introduction

Chapter 2 MightyWord Commands

Arithmetic

Borders

Copying Formats

Copying Text

Deleting Files

Deleting Text

⋮

Table of Contents

Tables

Tabs

Each area discussed will provide *all* information about that feature or command, with appropriate cross-references to related facilities.

Programming manuals

Many products—database products, languages, operating systems, programming environments, and others—are oriented toward developing software on top of those products. For example, a *database management system* (DBMS) may contain facilities to support a module language as well as an embedded code within a *third-generation language* (3GL).

In addition to user's guides and reference manuals, these products should have a manual for program developers. Discussions about program structure, compiling and linking options, parameter passing, memory management, and other programming-related issues should be discussed in enough detail to aid developers in using the product.

Coding examples should be included liberally. These examples should not be just small fragments with the particular statement or facility illustrated, but rather should include enough supplemental information—data types, flow control, program structure, and so forth—to provide a detailed picture for the reader.

Particular attention should be given to any areas of the language or product that are out of the ordinary; that is, they don't conform to traditional program structures or syntax families. For example, languages such as LISP and PROLOG, or expert systems shells with a great deal of behind-the-scenes processing, should have documentation that explains how statements are processed so that developers can write programs that function as they are expected to.

Programming manuals should also explain debugging features and tools, whether automated or manual.

Quick reference guides

We talked about "quick start" portions of user's guides earlier in this chapter. Quick reference guides are a similar concept, except that they often function in a standalone manner in the form of a foldout card or small booklet. The same features discussed above apply to the standalone forms.

Specialized guides

Systems that are particularly complex often have separate manuals, or at least separate sections in the users' documentation set, that deal with product installation, or steps required to begin using the product (configuration settings, and so on). These guides should be organized very precisely, step-by-step, with all possible configurations and permutations clearly noted. In some cases, completely separate (but somewhat repetitive) lists might be used. For example, if our sample MightyWord word processing package has different installation and start-up instructions for different types of local area networks, one format might be:

Chapter 2 LAN Installation
   To Install on a Novell NetWare LAN
   ——
   ——
   ——
   ——

To Install on a Banyan Vines LAN

——
——
——
——

A corresponding organization might be as follows:

Chapter 2 LAN Installation
   Step 1 Set User Permissions for Directories
      Novell NetWare

      ——
      ——

      Go to Step 2
      Banyan Vines

      ——
      ——

      Go to Step 2
   Step 2 Set Print Server Parameters
      Novell NetWare

      ——
      ——
      ——

      Go to Step 3
      Banyan Vines

      ——
      ——
      ——

      End Installation
   Step 3 Create Log-In Script (Novell NetWare Only)
      ——
      ——

      End Installation

Regardless of which form you decide to use, be sure that readers can follow your instructions to successfully complete the installation or initial configuration as necessary.

Maintenance manuals

Custom-developed software often is accompanied by a maintenance manual that is directed to those who must support the software. These manuals should carefully document all software dependencies and anything else that is required to support the software. Debugging and trouble-shooting guidelines should be presented as well.

Components of Documentation

Each of the different types of documentation above should conform to a document structure similar to that listed below:

1. *Title page.* Product or system name, version, date of documentation.
2. *Supporting information.* Document change history, address and/or phone number for comments and questions, related documents, and other supporting information.
3. *Table of contents.*
4. *The body of the documentation (user's manual, reference manual, and so on.).*
5. *Glossary of terms.* Any product- or system-specific term, as well as any other terms helpful in the use of the product, should be included.
6. *Appendices.* Any supplemental information that hasn't been included elsewhere in the documentation should be included here.
7. *Index.*

Guidelines for Preparing Documentation

Regardless of what forms of documentation you may be writing, you should follow these guidelines:

1. *Always ensure that documentation is updated.* There is a tendency, especially in situations where you informally make updates to custom software ("Hey, Sue, will you add a mailing label feature for me?"), to bypass updating documentation at that time. In most cases, documentation quickly becomes out of date as change after change becomes an "undocumented feature." Be sure that documentation is updated as changes occur, and don't forget to bill your client for those changes!

2. *Documentation should be tested along with software.* Large software systems, particularly commercial packages, undergo periods of internal and customer testing. It is usually desirable to field-test your documentation at the same time to obtain feedback as to its completeness, format, and usefulness.

3. *Use as many graphical examples as possible.* This is particularly true for GUI-based software, with a large number of menu bars, dialog boxes, on-screen buttons, and other GUI features. Most systems have a "screen capture" facility where a particular screen can be copied intact into a graphical file of some type (PostScript, a drawing program, or some other). Use of this type of facility can provide you with a comprehensive set of commands and features for your documentation.

4. *Have a section with troubleshooting information.* Most software and hardware documentation should have troubleshooting sections. This could be in the form of problems and suggested solutions. (Problem: The document won't output to the printer. Suggested solutions: (1) Be sure the printer is on-line, (2) Be sure the cable is installed correctly, and so forth). Alternatively, a Problem/Solution table might be appropriate.

5. *Provide detailed examples.* If you are writing a programming manual for a particular *fourth-generation language* (4GL) or database language, for example, you should express such facilities as procedure parameters and their data types in great detail. Additionally, examples should always be provided. For example, you might have:

```
Count_String_Length (String, Count)
where
String: input parameter, data type=string
Count: output parameter, data type=integer

Example

Employee_Name: String (20)
Length: Integer
    :
Count_String_Length, (Employee_Name, Length)
```

6. *Use annotations wherever feasible.* Some programming and reference manuals include lengthy code examples. In these situations, you might use symbols such as numeric bubbles or arrowed lines to annotate these code examples for further explanation. A code example with annotation is shown in Fig. 5.1.

7. *Always include safeguarding instructions.* Manuals that deal with conversions, migrations, upgrades, and other items should always include *extremely detailed* instructions as to the backup, safekeeping, and possible restoral of data and original software. These can be very important in the event of unforeseen problems, such as the user not having enough disk space, or system-related problems.

8. *Include a summary of new features.* Documentation that is being prepared for a new version of an existing product or system should have

---

Area_Code : String (3)
Numeric_Area_Code : Integer   ①
Phone_Number : String (13)
|
|
|
Get_Substring_(Phone_Number, 2, 3, Area_Code)   ②
*
*
String_to_Int (Area_Code, 3, Numeric_Area_Code)   ③

---

① Variable declaration must be done prior to function calls.

② All variable arguments to Get_Substring must be of type *String*.

③ The first argument must be the string to be converted, the second argument is the number of characters in that string, and the third argument must be of type *Integer*.

Figure 5.1 Annotation example.

an appendix or preface with a consolidated summary of new features, product changes, and any deletions. This summary will provide the experienced user with a quick guide to enhancements and revisions that he or she can use to rapidly become familiar with the new version.

Summary

The process of writing documentation can be a relatively straightforward process. User's manuals should tell users how to use a product or system; comprehensive reference manuals should provide a consolidated, complete list of all features; and so on. It is important to remember, however, that documentation is *not* a poor cousin to software or hardware, and in fact is every bit as much a part of a complete product or system as the hardware and software. By following relatively straightforward guidelines, any computer professional can produce documentation that serves his or her audience well.

Sample Documentation

A portion from a representative manual follows.

SimonWare
Version 2.0

Installation Guide
and
Reference Manual

A&J Software
Denver, Colorado

**READ THIS PAGE CAREFULLY--
YOU ARE AGREEING TO THE
LICENSING TERMS OF
SIMONWARE**

LICENSE AGREEMENT

*You would include appropriate
license agreement information here,
having to do with software ownership,
usage rights, etc.*

LIMITED WARRANTY

*You would include any warranty
information having to do with
magnetic media, what implied
warranties you are providing, the
<u>duration</u> of the warranty (typically
90 days), and other applicable
information.*

*Put any warranty and licensing information at the beginning
of your manual.*

Documentation-2

TABLE OF CONTENTS

One possible organization for your documentation.

INTRODUCTION

Welcome to Version 2.0 of SimonWare. The SimonWare tools help you edit files, perform calculator functions, and perform a number of other desktop functions. You can:

CREATE FILES

Create new files on distributed systems with varying operating systems, including UNIX, MS-DOS, Apple Macintosh, and others

EDIT FILES

Use a common text editing/word processing environment for any files, regardless of the system on which they reside

BACK UP FILES

Back up files from any or all of your environments with a single utility

INSERT CALCULATOR FUNCTIONS INTO WORD PROCESSING FILES

Use "hot key" operations to insert calculations into any word processing or text editing environment

"Sell" your product (or system) early in the documentation; others might read the documentation and find the product or system interesting enough to purchase their own.

Documentation-4

ABOUT THIS MANUAL

This installation guide and reference manual is divided into two sections. The first is the *QUICK REFERENCE GUIDE,* and is intended for users of SimonWare Version 1.2 or for those with extensive computer software experience. Product installation and basic usage functions are described in an abbreviated manner, with appropriate references to extensive discussion in the *REFERENCE MANUAL.*

The *REFERENCE MANUAL* includes detailed discussions of each of the features of SimonWare Version 2.0.

IMPORTANT!!!!!

If you are installing SimonWare Version 2.0 and will be using all system-provided defaults, you may follow the installation guidelines in the *QUICK REFERENCE GUIDE.* To perform any configuration functions - remote server installation, timed backup parameterization, or other advanced features - you MUST follow the installation guidelines found in the second section, *REFERENCE MANUAL.*

Throughout this manual, several notations are used:

• References to specific keys - the key name is surrounded by a ⬭ as in ⬭ENTER⬭ or ⬭ESCAPE⬭

• Menu commands are noted by a special font, as in

Open
Close
Save

Give the reader a roadmap to the documentation's organization.
Try to help the reader determine where in the manual he or she
should begin.

QUICK REFERENCE GUIDE

INSTALLATION

STOP...IF YOU WILL BE USING
THE PRESET DEFAULTS DURING
INSTALLATION, YOU MAY
PROCEED WITH THE FOLLOWING
SECTION. IF YOU WILL BE
PERFORMING YOUR OWN
CONFIGURATION, GO TO PAGE
3-1.

Step #1: You should have four 3 1/2 inch diskettes that
came with your SimonWare package:

- System Disk #1
- System Disk #2
- Utilities Disk #1
- Utilities Disk #2

Step #2: Determine whether you have at least 5 megabytes
of unused disk space available on your system.

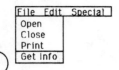

- Select Get Info from the File menu on the
  menu bar of your desktop. The pop-up window
  will show how much disk space is available for
  your use.

*Caution the reader again regarding whether he or she can use the particular
instructions on this page; if not, point to the appropriate place in the
documentation. Also, use icons and graphics - such as the image of a
diskette - when applicable.*

*Be very specific; leave nothing to chance regarding required system
configurations, etc.*   *Documentation-6*

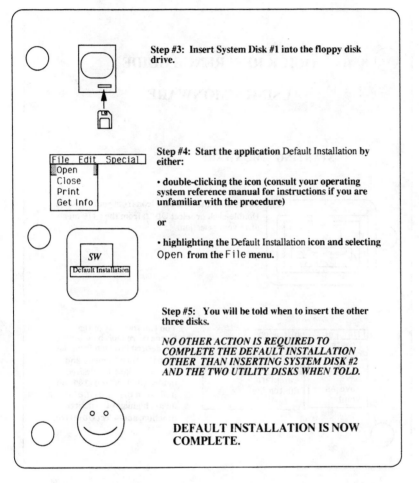

Step #3: Insert System Disk #1 into the floppy disk drive.

Step #4: Start the application Default Installation by either:

• double-clicking the icon (consult your operating system reference manual for instructions if you are unfamiliar with the procedure)

or

• highlighting the Default Installation icon and selecting Open from the File menu.

Step #5: You will be told when to insert the other three disks.

NO OTHER ACTION IS REQUIRED TO COMPLETE THE DEFAULT INSTALLATION OTHER THAN INSERTING SYSTEM DISK #2 AND THE TWO UTILITY DISKS WHEN TOLD.

DEFAULT INSTALLATION IS NOW COMPLETE.

QUICK REFERENCE GUIDE

USING SIMONWARE

STARTING SIMONWARE

Select the SimonWare 2.0 icon from your desktop.
Double-click or select Open from the File menu
after your selection.

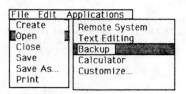

You can start any of the
SimonWare tools by selecting
the desired function from the
Applications menu and
double-clicking the desired
name. Alternatively, you can
pull down the Applications
menu, highlight the desired
function, and select Open from
the File menu.

Documentation-8

ERROR MESSAGES

There are two types of error messages you may receive while running SimonWare. The first type is errors from SimonWare, while the second type includes errors produced by your hardware or operating system software.

SimonWare errors are always preceded by the letters SW and a three-digit number, such as:

SW008 - Cannot find remote file
SW134 - Hot keys are inactive

This section includes a complete list of all errors produced by SimonWare.

Hardware and operating system errors are those outside the realm of SimonWare, such as disk errors, printer problems, and memory management errors. These types of errors vary according to the particular hardware and operating system environments you are connected to at the time the error occurs. These errors are *not* preceded by SW and the three-digit error number. Examples include:

Printer not ready - restart printer and press ENTER
Disk failure on Drive C: - cannot recover
Memory error at address 4D23E1

You must consult the appropriate system reference manual(s) for explanations of and corrections for these types of errors.

Many novice users aren't aware of the different types of errors, and may confuse operating system and hardware errors with those specifically handled by your software. A brief explanation can prevent customer misunderstandings.

Documentation-9

ERROR MESSAGES

SW001 - Requested File Does Not Exist

You requested access to a file that does not exist. Verify the file name - including all delimiters, version numbers, and other attributes - before retrying the function.

SW002 - Could Not Access Remote System

You attempted to access a remote system that did not respond. The remote system may be unavailable due to system failure, lack of available connections, or another reason.

SW003 - Could Not Save File - Insufficient Space

You attempted to save a file to a disk device that has insufficient available space for your file. You must try another disk device or delete a sufficient number of files to provide you with adequate storage space.

SW004 - Requested Operation Is Not Supported

You attempted to perform a remote operation that is not supported by the remote system. You must retry the operation on another system or select another operation.

SW005 - Customization Failed

You attempted to perform a customization function that was unsuccessful. Recheck all parameters before trying again.

If you have a moderate number of error messages, you may choose to list them alphabetically or in numerical sequence. If you have a large number of messages without any type of ordering mechanism, you may choose to group them by function (all disk errors together, all menu choice errors together, etc.).

Documentation-10

Whenever possible, offer solutions to the error.

6

Writing Requests for Proposals (RFPs)

Introduction

"Hey, Sue . . . have you got a minute?"

"Sure, Jim. What's up?"

"Well, we need to have an inventory management system developed. Would you like to send us a proposal?"

"OK, Jim. I'll get it to you sometime in the next couple of weeks."

"Great. Thanks, Sue."

Though some information-systems-development proposals are solicited in a somewhat informal manner, as illustrated above, most requests to submit proposals are made through a document that bears that name: *Request for Proposal,* or an RFP. In many environments, particularly those involving local, state, or federal government organizations, RFPs are a *required* component of the information-systems-procurement process. That is, most acquisitions must be done on a competitive basis, with proposals submitted in response to an RFP.

Even in commercial environments, more and more organizations have adopted an RFP process, particularly as the size and complexity of the systems being acquired increase. While commercial environments usually aren't as restrictive as governmental ones with respect to the required contents and format of RFPs, the procedure still has a great deal of merit, if only to provide a comprehensive requirements list to one or more prospective suppliers.

In this chapter, we'll look at the contents and format of RFP documents. There are several items to keep in mind:

1. In most governmental environments, there are strict guidelines that govern the contents and format of RFP documents. The documents must always contain certain sections, paragraphs must be numbered in a given manner; a certain set of evaluation criteria must be used, and so on. Even in these circumstances, the general guidelines discussed in this chapter with respect to word usage and other topics will still be valuable to those who must write, review, and approve RFPs.

2. There are "cousin" documents to RFPs, such as the *Request for Information* (RFI) and *Request for Quotation* (RFQ). As the name suggests, RFIs are used as a pre-RFP means to seek information. Organizations who aren't ready to begin a formal procurement process, but wish to gather technical information, may issue an RFI to prospective bidders for a response along the lines of, "If you were to put together a system today to meet these requirements, how would you do it?" RFQs are used primarily for off-the-shelf procurements with few, if any, integration requirements, and practically no development. That is, providing prices for only specified items, rather than submitting proposals with competitive solutions that are evaluated against each other.

Disclaimer: This chapter is intended as a guide for writing an RFP, rather than as a tutorial or instruction manual on competitive procurement processes. Where necessary, we try to explain basic terminology where particular concepts are important to understanding how to develop an RFP. There are, however, many more aspects to the competitive procurement process, evaluation, and selection criteria, and other areas that are beyond the scope of this chapter.

Many computer professionals who have been involved in an RFP process, either as an issuer or a respondent, find that the follow-up activities often become confrontational with respect to success or failure in meeting requirements and other aspects of competitive procurement. *If possible, RFPs should be written in a manner that fosters a partnership between the eventual successful bidder and the issuer.* By attempting to eliminate ambiguities, include comprehensive requirements, and by following other guidelines presented in this chapter, a great deal of potential conflict can be reduced or eliminated among parties. Then the goal of the RFP—securing information system components that meet requirements at a reasonable cost—can become the primary focal point rather than being obscured by a confrontational environment.

Word Usage

It is very important that words, phrases, and terminology be carefully selected and, if necessary, explained within an RFP. Imperative words such as "shall"—which, according to the dictionary[1] means "will have to" or "must," are used to *require* certain performance criteria. It is unlikely that an RFP writer would include a sentence such as, "It would be nice if the system can [perform some function]"; to avoid conflict in determining which features are mandatory and which are optional, explicit mention of such requirements should be stated in imperative language.

Even more important is that all terms that may have multiple meanings (and, of course, there are plenty of those in the computer industry) be fully explained. For example, a request to supply a "distributed database" without any expansion on the term might yield proposed systems anywhere from one with remote access to data to one that performs distributed units of work under a distributed concurrency-control algorithm. Even terms such as "schema" and "database" should be explained. What kind of database model (relational? object-oriented?); what is the definition of the word "schema"?; etc.

Acronyms without prior explanation should be avoided. The acronym "GUI" might stand for *graphical user interface* or, in some other term, be an abbreviation for a system name such as "Guaranteed Uniform Integration." "CD" (as in a "CD Information Retrieval System") might stand for context dispatcher, compact diskette, certificate of deposit. To avoid controversy, and to simplify the accompanying procurement process, any doubt as to the meaning of terms should be removed.

Establishing Requirements

The primary purpose of the RFP is to solicit one or more proposals for the evaluation and selection of candidate technologies to meet the requirements at hand. It is extremely important to this process that the RFP *carefully* specify exact criteria that the proposal must meet. This means that not only must any ambiguity be removed (see above), but that an exhaustive list of all requirements be included.

The classes of requirements to be included in an RFP include:

Features. A certain set of features is inherent in the commercial software, custom software, hardware, training, and other technologies that are being acquired. Whether the features are "participating in the XYZ two-phase commit algorithm" or "an operator reset button shall be prominently displayed on the graphical user screen," the rule for RFPs is that *no list of features is too small*. That is, any and all features should be listed in the appropriate RFP section.

We recommend two cautions with respect to features lists. First, be sure that the features lists in different parts of the RFP do not conflict with one another. That is, a requirement that "all system software shall permit use of the ABC word processing package in place of the native text editor" should not be contradicted by a requirement elsewhere in the RFP that states, "Security Requirement: No external software, such as word processors or query languages, shall be used with the transaction log." All such inconsistencies should be resolved *before the RFP is issued to prospective proposal submitters.*

Second, there is a tendency to build a "wish list" of features into the RFP requirements. As we discussed in Chap. 2, with developed software there is a cost for every feature and component that goes into a completed system; if they are deemed worthy, however, an exhaustive list of features can be included in an RFP with cost proposals expected to be correspondingly higher than those for a smaller set of features. For *commercial software,* however, the wish list process presents a major problem. One of the authors once worked on a proposal in response to a U.S. Government Department of Defense RFP for commercial office software (word processing, spreadsheet, electronic mail, and so on). The features list for each software component had been developed from a composite of specifications sheets of the many commercial packages available in each area; if spreadsheet package No.1 had features A, B, and C, and spreadsheet package No.2 had features C, D, and E, the RFP requirements list for spreadsheet software had A, B, C, D, and E. While it surely was desirable to have as complete a spreadsheet package as possible, the reality in nearly every software area was that no single commercial package contained all of the features listed in the RFP. Our solution was to work with software vendors and attempt to have features added to their commercial packages, but this was exceedingly difficult (and exceedingly expensive in terms of the cost proposal), especially since we were working with large well-known vendors. *When preparing the RFP features list, reality should play a role when including various features, especially for those that are only peripherally important.*

Performance.   All response times and other time-oriented measures must be mentioned explicitly in the RFP. For example, statements such as the following should be included:

- "A file with 10,000 records shall be sorted in ascending order using two alphabetic and one numeric field as sort keys. Each record shall contain a minimum of ten fields, and no fields shall be null-valued or zero-valued."

- "A user request to query the database shall result in a 'WORKING: PLEASE STAND BY' message within 0.4 seconds of pressing the ENTER key."

- "Completed context switches within the window management program shall occur in 0.5 seconds' time or less. A context switch is completed when all overlapping windows are repainted and the pointing device can accept user input."

Note, for example, that often it isn't enough just to say, "the file shall be sorted within four minutes," since a file can take many formats in terms of number of records, number of fields per record, applicable indices that must be readjusted, the values (or lack thereof) within the file's records, and other factors. It is especially important for the *live test demonstrations* (LTDs, discussed later) that these items be explicitly noted for all respondents, to ensure level playing fields and equal comparisons among candidate solutions.

Response Criteria

An important part of the RFP is the specification of all response criteria for prospective proposal submitters. Response criteria include:

1. *The deadline date and time.* Example: "4:00 P.M. Eastern Daylight Time, Monday, October 14, 1991."

2. *The place of submission.* "Received at IOU Corporate Headquarters, 1212 Main Street, New York, NY, 10000, 4th Floor, Information Systems Department."

3. *The mode of transmission.* If the deadline date is not an "in our hands" deadline (and therefore the mode of transmission doesn't matter as long as it is there), the mode of transmission may be stated as "Postmarked or received by an overnight courier service by [. . . deadline date and, if applicable, time]." Special case: If electronic submissions are acceptable through a shared network or via modem, the RFP should state as such, along with appropriate deadlines, electronic mail addresses, and other necessary information.

4. *The media of the proposal.* "The proposal shall be submitted on 8½" × 11" paper, with all pages enclosed in one or more bound two- or three-ring binders . Additionally, the entire proposal, including graphics and cost data, shall be submitted on one or more 800-kb 3½" diskettes readable by Apple Macintosh systems. All text shall be in either TIWQ Word Processing software format or in ASCII text. All graphics shall be in FGHJ Drawing software format. All spreadsheet-based cost data shall be in XYZ Spreadsheet software format."

5. *Policies regarding missed deadlines and other discrepancies.* If any grace periods are possible, the RFP should explicitly state as such; nothing invites a legal protest (in government procurements) as much as the perception that deadlines are extended in favor of indi-

vidual vendors. Similarly, for minor discrepancies—such as the word processing files for electronic transmission are unreadable—the policies should be clearly stated.

6. *Policies regarding alternative solutions.* We will discuss this issue a bit more in the next chapter while dealing with proposals. To reduce the amount of confusion during the evaluation process, there should be a clear statement among the response criteria as to whether alternative solutions to issuer-supplied requirements will be permitted.

7. *Any limitations on page size.* Some RFPs explicitly express a page limit to one or more sections of the responding proposals to help weed out extraneous material that has little or no substance. For example: "Each section of responding proposals to this RFP shall contain no more pages than the number specified below:

Section	Page count
Technical	100
Cost	25
Company Qualifications	5
Development Schedule	10

Selection and Evaluation Criteria

Each RFP should state explicitly how the submitted proposals will be evaluated and rated, and how the final selection will be made. This usually is required in government procurements, and is recommended for commercial procurements as well in order to fairly *and effectively* govern the selection process. Several evaluation areas factor into the competitive selection process, including:

1. *Cost.* We will discuss cost criteria in more detail later. The selection and evaluation criteria should state explicitly:

   - Whether or not this procurement automatically will be awarded to the lowest cost bidder
   - If low cost is not the automatic decision point, how cost figures into the selection equation (in explicit percentage)
   - Whether current or present-value dollars (explained later) are used
   - Whether expected-value costing (also explained later) is used

2. *Technical criteria.* The RFP should state explicitly whether the technical evaluation is of:

- "Pass or fail" format—that is, each and every requirement must be met, or the proposal is automatically rejected.
- What percentage of a combined evaluation (along with cost and other factors) goes to technical merit; this can be further be subdivided along the lines of "20% of the total score will be based on PC software evaluation; 30% of the total score will be based on network technology evaluation. . . . "
- If not of "pass or fail" format, how the technical merits of the competing proposals will be judged, including relative importance of the *live test demonstration* (LTD, discussed later).

3. *Company-specific factors.* These include the stability, references, and other attributes of the companies submitting proposals, including the relative technical qualifications of their development staffs, and other such factors.

4. *Negative factors.* If items of "negative history" (example: having failed to meet development deadlines on a similar system in the past) will be included in the evaluation criteria, these *may* (note the use of an "optional" word) be included along with the "positive" selection criteria.

Avoiding Protest Activity

No, this does not mean calling out the National Guard. In our context of RFPs, proposals, and competitive procurement processes, we are referring to protests regarding the contents of RFPs, as well as protests that contest the contract award. This issue primarily concerns government procurements, which, as we discussed earlier, have voluminous sets of rules and regulations.

Much of the responsibility in avoiding protest rests with the author or authors of the RFPs. By (1) carefully following any and all rules regarding the content, format, and other facets of the RFP, (2) carefully choosing reasonable and appropriate selection and evaluation criteria from the alternatives available, and (3) ensuring that numbers (1) and (2) above are reflected in the body of the RFP (as well as in all related activities), a great deal of potential for problems can be eliminated. There are also many activities outside the specifics of the RFP itself, such as what communication is and isn't permitted among procurement personnel, users, and the competing bidders; but these are outside the scope of this book. As we mentioned at the beginning of this chapter, RFPs are but a single part of the procurement process, though they are an important one.

Cost Criteria

We discussed above how cost criteria should be stated explicitly in the RFP's selection and evaluation criteria. Let's look a bit further at various ways cost can be evaluated, and how they should be reflected in an RFP.

Simple, one-time procurements can be done on a *current dollar* basis. That is, there is no need to handle multiple years of cash flows, nor (in the simplest cases) does any type of expected value factor need to be considered. In these cases, the RFP should state simply that the cost basis presented in the proposal will be used in the evaluation criteria. This is applicable whether the procurement is a cost-only one or whether cost is but one of the selection factors.

Multiple-year procurements, however, should be calculated on a *present value* basis. This means that a dollar received today is worth more than a dollar received a year from now, because the dollar received today could earn interest to make it worth, say $1.06 at the point that the other dollar is received in the future. Conversely, next year's dollar may be worth only $.94 today, since that amount could have been invested and be worth one dollar at that future point.

Confused? Just remember this simple rule: For multiple-year procurements, with cash expenditures staged over various periods, present-value analysis should be used—or at least considered—*and stated as such in the RFP.* Let's look at the following example: Suppose you write an RFP to solicit proposals for a custom inventory management system. Vendor A and Vendor B both bid $1 million worth of software development and associated hardware. Vendor A's costs are placed nearer to the present time in the development life cycle, while Vendor B's costs are placed near the end of, for example, a three-year development time. Even though the dollar amounts are identical, Vendor A's bid is actually higher than Vendor B's due to the present value of the cash flows and associated expenses.

Again, the point is, regardless of whether a present-value or current-dollar basis is used, the evaluation policy should be clearly stated in the RFP.

Another variation on cost evaluation that should be reflected in the RFP is the use of expected-value costing, in conjunction with either present-value or current-dollar costing. Assume that the RFP being written is for a large number of hardware and commercial software items, some of which are certain to be acquired, while others may or may not be procured. Additionally, the RFP may state that 2500 copies of a word processing package should be bid and costed, but that only 1500 are certain to be ordered over the next two years; the additional 1000 may or may not be purchased in years three and four of the contract life. One possibility is that a *probability assessment* may be assigned to the acquisition of each item; the associated cost is multiplied by the probability and factored into the overall cost structure. For example:

Item	Probability	Present-value total cost	Expected-value total cost
1000 word processing packages	100%	$100,000	$100,000
500 word processing packages	75%	$ 45,000	$ 33,750
Word processing file servers	50%	$120,000	$ 60,000
		Total evaluated cost	$193,750

Expected-value costing attempts to take into account the probabilities of acquiring certain items. If there is only a 10% chance of acquiring a specific high-cost item, the overall cost structures of the responding proposals may be blurred by that particular entry, which can distort the overall true-cost picture. Assume that a single item is bid by Vendor A at $1 million and Vendor B at $2 million, but there is only a 10% chance of actually acquiring this item. If the rest of Vendor A's cost proposal is $ 1.2 million but Vendor B's is $0.6 million, Vendor A's overall proposal may be valued at $2.2 million, while that of Vendor B appears to be more expensive at a total cost of $2.6 million. By taking into account the probability of acquiring that one item, the following evaluation appears:

Vendor A: (100% × $1.2 million) + (10% × $1 million) = $1.3 million expected value

Vendor B: (100% × $0.6 million) + (10% × $2 million) = $0.8 million expected value

Using this analysis, there is a *probability* that Vendor B's solution will have a lower overall cost, given the uncertainty of whether a high-ticket item will have to be acquired. Again, this is not intended as a primer on procurement policies. The point, as with present-value costing, is that the RFP should state clearly what cost evaluation policies are operative.

Tip: Given the confusion likely on the two items above among many non-financial people in the computer field, RFPs should include sample tables and/or templates into which the cost figures can be placed; this will help to avoid confusion among recipients of the RFP and should lessen the likelihood of subsequent legal challenges.

Live Test Demonstrations (LTDs)

Many programs, particularly large-scale ones, that are solicited through the RFP process are accompanied by vendor demonstrations of their proposed systems; these are sometimes known as *live test demonstrations,* or LTDs. The purposes of the LTD include:

- Demonstrating the feasibility of the technical solution proposed.
- Permitting hands-on evaluation of the proposed systems by the acquisition person or team.
- Providing an atmosphere—important in government procurements—in which the vendor, the users, and the acquisition team can exchange ideas in a controlled manner. Note that in many government procurements there are extensive restrictions on which communications are and aren't permitted among the parties involved.

All policies and criteria related to LTDs should be discussed in the RFP. For example, a section in the RFP relating to the LTD should include:

- *The time frame of the LTD during the procurement process.* Given that multiple vendors will be likely to respond to the RFP, there should be a window of time wide enough to accommodate the expected number of responses. For example, if each LTD will last four days, and five vendors are expected to submit proposals, a six-week window and accompanying dates should be listed in the RFP. This window will allow for one week per vendor (four demonstration days plus travel days) plus an additional week either for recovery from travel or to accommodate an additional bidder.

- *The required items that will be included in the LTD.* It is unlikely that each and every requirement listed in the body of the RFP will be evaluated, due to time limitations, logistics, and so on. Particularly in cases of large-scale software development, the evaluation during an LTD will most likely be on a proof-of-concept prototype of certain portions of the target system.

- *Any requirements for a remote test generator.* Many LTDs use a *remote test data generator* to emulate distributed aspects of a system under evaluation; this might include large numbers of users, distributed remote operations, and similar functions. RFPs should state explicitly the characteristics (interfaces, required functions, and so forth) of remote test generators.

- *Characteristics of stress-test and performance evaluations.* As with RFP requirements themselves, performance evaluations should be stated explicitly in terms of file sizes and contents and other factors. If standardized test data provided by the RFP writer will be used, the format (operating system, media, and so on), and other facets of the test data should listed in the RFP.

Other Characteristics of RFPs

There are other aspects of RFPs that should be considered or included among the contents. These are:

1. *New hardware and software versions.* If upwardly compatible versions of commercial software and hardware are to be provided by vendors when available, the RFP should specify this. For example, if word processing package WriteRightWrite Version 2.0 is bid by Vendor A, there may be a requirement to replace all 500 copies with Version 2.5 when it comes on the market. Associated costs, including file conversions and other overhead (such as changing GUI menu choices for all users), should be specified by bidders in their proposals, and in turn should be prompted by the RFP request for new version items.

2. *Software and hardware maintenance.* All RFPs should include line-item requests for maintenance of all items.

3. *Legal ownership.* For items such as developed software, ownership of software and other legal facets (licensing agreements, and so forth) should be clearly specified in the RFP.

4. *Legal penalties.* Many RFPs include payment penalties for missed deadlines and other situations of nonperformance. If any penalties will be enforced, they must be *clearly and explicitly* stated in the RFP.

5. *Vendor qualifications.* We mentioned briefly that company qualifications of those responding with proposals may be an evaluation factor. In many situations, particularly those involving complex software development, the RFP issuer specifies minimum qualifications for the bidders' proposed development personnel. This helps ensure that competitive costs are not excessively skewed by having one vendor propose, for example, 40 entry-level personnel at a much lower cost than a competitor's 40 people with an average of 10 years of experience each. While RFP issuers should be concerned only with the final results, it may be their opinion that for particular programs a *certain experience level,* with specific training in software engineering, could help reduce the risk associated with the development efforts. This might include training in the chosen

development languages (such as Ada), and other technologies (example: distributed database applications development).

6. *Integration requirements.* If the proposed system must be integrated with existing hardware or software, any requirements or acceptable means of integration should be included in the RFP. These include network integration (protocols, acceptable bridges and gateways, performance throughput requirements, and so on), software integration (software bridges, interoperability products, file transfer capabilities and protocols, application-to-application integration, federated distributed database integration, and so on), and other means. If the successful bidder must make any modifications on the RFP issuer's *existing* system in order to meet integration requirements, these should be included in the proposals in response to explicit mention in the RFP.

7. *All peripheral activities.* In addition to specific software and hardware items, there are often a number of peripheral, associated activities that are easy to overlook which may be included in an RFP. These might include:

- Preparation of user scripts, log-in facilities, passwords, and permissions (for local area network or multiuser systems)
- Inclusion of software programs as menu choices for all users
- System administration and management "canned" facilities, such as backup and recovery scripts
- Conversion of existing data files or databases to meet new formats

Amendments to RFPs

No matter how carefully an RFP is prepared, reviewed, and modified prior to issuance, there probably will be later amendments as vendors have questions and find inconsistencies, or as budgets and other elements change during the procurement cycle. Amendments that change various aspects of RFPs should be issued in a timely *and consistent* (to all recipients simultaneously) manner. Amendments can include changes to requirements, proposal submission schedule, and other factors. *It is strongly recommended that major changes, such as radical modifications in evaluation criteria and inclusion of major new system components, be avoided in the amendment process, particularly in tightly controlled governmental procurement environments.* Changing the evaluation criteria three weeks before proposals are due, for example, is likely to incite protests and legal challenges from unsuccessful bidders, who might claim that the evaluation criteria were changed to favor the eventual winner. If major changes are unavoidable, consider-ation should be given to withdrawing a particular RFP and reissuing a modified, brand new one.

Summary

The next chapter discusses several types of proposals, including those submitted in response to RFPs. There is a strong correlation between the quality of such proposals and the quality of the RFP to which they are responding. The more complete an RFP and the less ambiguous the various sections are, the better the resulting proposals will be. Many computer professionals, particularly those specializing in systems acquisition, have experience writing both RFPs and proposals. There is a complementary relationship between the associated processes. Those who have developed processes in response to unclear RFPs usually gain an appreciation for what a "good" RFP should contain. Conversely, those writers of RFPs who review many proposals gain insights into which qualities are desirable, and which "work" in proposals.

End Note

1. *Webster's New Collegiate Dictionary*, 1975, p. 1064.

Sample RFP

A sample RFP ends this chapter. We have included as many of the items discussed in this chapter as possible. Note that not all items are applicable to each and every procurement situation. The sample RFP should be reviewed with an eye for format and organization rather than technical content.

Raised numbers within the body of the sample RFP correspond to comments found in the RFP End Notes.

Request for Proposals

Michaelson Electronics, Inc.

Office Information System

RFP #1215   Issued by:

Date Issued: Michaelson Electronics, Inc.
  February 15, 1992   1212 Waterbridge Avenue
Proposals Due: Phoenix, AZ 85200
  May 31, 1992   (602) 555-0000

1   Introduction and Executive Summary

Michaelson Electronics, Inc. is soliciting proposals from qualified vendors in response to this *Request for Proposal* (RFP) for an *office information system* (OIS). The technical aspects of the OIS are described in Section 2 of this RFP. The OIS shall contain:

- Word processing capabilities
- Distributed database management system (DDBMS) capabilities
- Graphics software and "slide show" presentation capabilities
- System administration and network management capabilities
- Local area network (LAN) hardware, interface devices, and software
- Vendor development of inventory management applications software

Additionally, each proposal responding to this RFP shall contain costs for training and maintenance, as outlined in Section 2 of this RFP.

2   Technical Description

1   Overview

The OIS shall contain hardware, commercially available software, and custom software capable of supporting all requirements outlined in this RFP. Each Michaelson Electronics user of the OIS shall have a personal desktop computer, meeting the following minimum characteristics:

- MS-DOS 3.31 or greater
- 80386 or 80486 processor
- clock speed of 16 MHz or faster
- hard disk of 80 Mb or greater capacity
- a minimum 1.5 Mb of main memory
- LookAtMe V2.5 window and task management software

All software proposed by respondents to this RFP shall run in a standalone environment on a desktop computer meeting the above minimum configuration. Additionally, the Inventory Management applications software shall operate in a client/server model, with the client portion operating on a desktop system meeting the above minimum configuration, and the server portion operating on remote hardware connected via a local area network (LAN) to client systems.

2 Word processing software

Word processing capabilities shall be delivered for 500 simultaneous users. Any configuration—LAN Server-based, individual copy, midrange-based, or other—that meets the requirements listed below is acceptable.

a Simultaneous use and availability.   Each user shall be able to invoke the word processing software and all functions at any time, subject to availability of his or her desktop computer. Downtime for file backup, administrative functions, maximum number of users, or other reasons other than hardware failure, is not permissible. No performance degradation as a result of other users' activities shall affect any individual user's software performance.

b Windowed environment.   The word processing software shall be capable of operating in one or more windows under LookAtMe V2.5 window and task management software. Each user shall be able to have up to ten windows open simultaneously. Each window shall provide access to an entire word processing document or to a portion of a document open at the same time in another window. Context switches to another word processing window, as defined by the user clicking his or her mouse on the window of choice and being able to enter text or perform other operations in the newly current window, shall take no longer than 0.5 seconds.

c Presentation capabilities.   The word processing software shall be capable of the following presentation characteristics:

(1) Inclusion of editable graphics from the graphics software proposed in compliance with Section 2.4 of this RFP. Graphics images shall scroll together with text, and the graphics software shall be able to be invoked from the word processing software through the trigger interface of the LookAtMe V2.5 window and task management software.

(2) Screen presentation of the following fonts and textual attributes:[1]

Fonts

Times

Helvetica

Bookman

Palatino

Text sizes

9 point

10 point

12 point

14 point

18 point

24 point

Textual attributes

Solid underline

Word-only underline

Double underline

~~Strike-through~~

Boldface

Italics

d Document size. The word processing software shall be capable of editing a document of up to 100 MB in size, regardless of the amount of available memory in the user's desktop system. All virtual document management, defined as swapping segments of any document between memory and disk, shall be performed by the word processing software without user action or intervention.

e Subwindows. Each word processing window shall be capable of being split into two or more "subwindows." Each subwindow shall be immediately accessible within 0.5 seconds by use of the mouse or another pointing device to select the subwindow.

f Spelling verification. The word processing software shall have a built-in spelling verification system with a built-in dictionary containing at least 75,000 words. Each user shall be capable of creating a personal dictionary. Built-in and personal dictionaries shall both be consulted by the word processing spelling verification system without the user having to specifically request which dictionary shall be consulted. The spelling verification system shall have a "suggestion" mode where likely candidates to replace an incorrect word are presented to the user for selection. The spelling verification system shall have the capability to ignore words with all capital letters, and this capability shall be user-selectable.

g Physical document size. The word processing software shall be capable of supporting physical document sizes up to 35″ wide.

h Margins. Left and right margins shall be selectable in either inches or centimeters.

i Tabs. Users shall be able to select an unlimited number of left, right, center, and decimal tabs.

3 Distributed database management system

The OIS shall contain a *distributed database management system* (DDBMS) upon which applications and query capabilities will be developed. The inventory management system specified in Section 2.7 shall be built on top of the DDBMS. The DDBMS shall support all of the requirements listed below:

a Remote access. Any user shall be capable of retrieving data from a remote node without having to specify the node to the DDBMS query system, to an application program, or in any other manner.

b Distributed partitions. The DDBMS shall support both horizontal and vertical partitions, as defined in Appendix B of this RFP.[2] The *data definition language* (DDL) shall provide facilities for specification by users or *database administrators* (DBAs) of the partitioning parameters. All global operations shall be performed without the need to specify the location of partitions or to request that partitions be regrouped.

c Distributed concurrency control. The DDBMS shall support distributed concurrency control and distributed locking algorithms to ensure that data integrity is maintained across the global database environment.[3] Distributed locking algorithms shall support both timeout and deadlock resolution mechanisms.

d Rollback. The DDBMS shall support distributed rollback of a transaction in progress to the state prior to the beginning of the transaction. All data and metadata at all nodes shall be restored to their state at the time prior to the beginning of the transaction. No other simultaneous transactions shall be affected by the rollback.

e Metadata management. All DDBMS metadata definitions shall be stored in a centralized repository.

f Language. The DDBMS language shall support all features of the SQL-92 standard, Level 2.

g Distributed security. The DDBMS shall support two levels of security:

(1) Authorization of users through the SQL-92 GRANT and REVOKE statements

(2) Authentication of remote nodes

4 Graphics and presentation management software

Graphics and presentation capabilities shall be delivered for 500 simultaneous users. Any configuration—LAN Server-based, individual copy, midrange-based, or other—that meets the requirements listed below is acceptable.

a Supported graphics. The graphics software shall be capable of automatically creating the following types of graphs from selected input data:

- Bar
- Pie
- Line
- Column

b Annotations. Users shall have the capability of selecting and modifying annotations on any graphical data item, along with vertical and horizontal axis titles.

c Data Input. The graphics software shall be capable of accepting input from the DDBMS proposed in response to Section 2.3 of this RFP. Additionally, input data from CalcVille spreadsheet software shall be automatically processed through cut and paste operations under LookAtMe V2.5 window and task management software at each user's desktop personal computer.

d   Colors.   Users shall be able to select from a palette of 256 colors. Any individual item within the graphics software—data items, annotations, shadings, horizontal axis, vertical axis—shall be capable of individual selection of its color from the palette.

e   Slide show capabilities.   Users shall be able to create and play a "slide show" of graphics screens. The slide show shall permit forward and backward scrolling, adjustable time intervals for automatic scrolling, and automatic modification of slide ordering.

5   System and network administration and management

The OIS shall have a system and network administration and management ("Management") capability. This capability shall include:

a   Distributed backup.   The *system administrator* (SA) shall be able to back up part or all of the OIS from a single location within the OIS. Full and incremental backups shall be supported by the Management. The SA shall be have the capability to specify that incremental backups be performed on a "SINCE [time]" or "on CHANGE" basis, as defined in Appendix D.[4]

b   Integrated backup.   The Management shall support backups of the DDBMS partitions within the context of the system backup.

c   Utilities.   The following utilities and system management capabilities shall be included:[5]

- Device allocation and deallocation
- Password management
- Network security
- Accounting
- Print resource management
- Dump analysis
- Capacity alarms
- Image snapshot

6   Local area network (LAN)

Each user desktop computer shall be connected to a local area network (LAN). Any topology and protocol set is permissible, provided response and access requirements are supported.[6]

a   Interface devices.   Interface devices, with applicable hardware and software, are required for 500 desktop personal computers matching the minimum specifications listed in Section 2.1.

b   Cabling.   Appendix E contains the floor plan, raceway location, and other building information for Michaelson Electronics. Sufficient cabling shall be proposed to meet the LAN requirements.

c   Integrated management.   All LAN management capabilities shall be integrated into and callable from the system management functions described in Section 2.5.

7   Inventory management (IM) applications software

The respondent shall propose technical and cost solutions to develop an *inventory management* (IM) software environment for Michaelson Electronics. The IM software shall use the DDBMS proposed in compliance with Section 2.3 as the underlying data manager. The IM software shall meet all requirements listed below.

a   Just-in-time management.   The IM software shall support just-in-time inventory algorithms defined in Appendix H.[7]

b   User interface.   The IM software shall be callable from and managed under the windowing environment of LookAtMe V2.5 window and task management software.

c   Reports.   The IM software shall produce the following reports:[8]

- Finished goods inventory report
- Work in progress inventory report
- Cost accounting variance report
- Order transaction report

8 Training

The vendor shall provide the following training to Michaelson Electronics users:

	Course	Est. length
Introduction to Word Processing	1 day	15
Advanced Word Processing	3 days	10
Introduction to Graphics	2 days	15
Introduction to Database Operations	2 days	15
Advanced DDBMS Support	5 days	5
IM Software Training	5 days	10

3 Schedule

The schedule for the development and submission of proposals responding to this RFP and the required system-acquisition milestones, are listed below. All organizations to whom this RFP is being sent will be notified automatically of any and all modifications to the schedule. Requests for modifications to the schedule must be addressed in writing to:

Michaelson Electronics, Inc.
Attn: Ms. Ann Lucas
1212 Waterbridge Avenue
Phoenix, AZ 85200

Each request must state (1) the requested change of date, and (2) the reason for the modification request. The requestor will be notified in writing within five calendar days of the approval or denial of the request. All other recipients of this RFP will automatically be notified in writing within four calendar days.

February 15, 1992: Issuance of RFP #1215

May 31, 1992: Responding proposals due to Michaelson Electronics, per submission criteria listed in Section 4 of this RFP.

June 1–July 15, 1992: Initial evaluation of proposals; issuance of questions, requests for clarification, and *discrepancy reports* (DRs) to respondents

July 16–August 15, 1992: *Live test demonstration* (LTD) period; see Section 6 for further details.

August 15–September 15, 1992: Final evaluation of proposals and LTD results

September 16, 1992: Award of OIS contract

4 Submission Criteria for Proposals

All proposals are due by 4:00 P.M., May 31, 1992 to Michaelson Electronics, Inc., at the following address:

Michaelson Electronics, Inc.
Attn: Ms. Ann Lucas
1212 Waterbridge Avenue
Phoenix, AZ 85200

Three copies of each proposal shall be submitted, with each in a separate binder. Proposals shall be on 8½″ × 11″ paper. Foldout pages for schedule charts and large diagrams are permitted.

No late submissions shall be considered by Michaelson Electronics.

5 Evaluation Criteria

Proposals submitted in response to this RFP shall be evaluated as follows:

Cost		50%
Technical		40%
IM software	15%	
LAN	10%	
Word processing	5%	
Graphics	5%	
System management	5%	
Vendor qualifications		10%

6 Live Test Demonstration (LTD)

Each submission of a proposal shall be accompanied by a *live test demonstration* (LTD) of the proposed solution. The LTD shall be three days in length and shall consist of the following portions:

1. *IM prototype software demonstration.* Each vendor shall develop a small-scale prototype of the IM software, compliant with the specifications listed in Appendix J.[9]

2. *Word processing software demonstration.* Each vendor shall demonstrate the capabilities of its proposed word processing software solution. No canned script shall be provided by Michaelson Electronics, so the demonstration can be free-format.

3.. *Graphics software demonstration.* Each vendor shall demonstrate the capabilities of its proposed graphics and presentation software solution. No canned script shall be provided by Michaelson Electronics, so the demonstration can be free-format.

4. *Distributed database software demonstration.* Each vendor shall demonstrate the capabilities of its proposed distributed database management system (DDBMS) solution. The DDBMS demonstration shall utilize a remote test data generator to emulate remote nodes. All distributed database operations shall interact with the remote test data generator. The remote test data generator shall be capable of supporting the distributed concurrency control algorithm.

7   Vendor Experience

A portion of the evaluation criteria for the OIS, as noted in Section 5, will be based on the past and proposed qualifications of the candidates. Evaluation criteria shall include:

1. Demonstrated vendor experience with similar environments to the Michaelson Electronics OIS.

2. Qualifications of proposed IM software developers.

Each proposal shall include a maximum of five pages detailing vendor qualifications, including customer references, software developers' experience levels and backgrounds, and other information deemed important by the proposal submitter.

8   Legal

Michaelson Electronics shall receive ownership of the IM software upon successful installation and acceptance testing. All commercial software proposed for the OIS shall conform to industry-standard licensing practices.[10]

RFP End Notes

1. Whenever possible, include specific graphical examples in the body of the RFP, such as we have done with fonts, type sizes, and textual attributes. This helps prevent problems caused by misunderstanding: for example, the typeface of a specific font. The widespread use of laser printers has greatly enhanced these demonstrative capabilities within the body of the RFP itself.
2. The appendix (not included within) would contain explanatory and graphical examples of partitions, both horizontal and vertical, and describe the respective manners under which the partitions are created and managed.
3. This particular section deliberately is written somewhat vaguely so as not to prejudice the technical solutions proposed. It would be tempting to specify that "the DDBMS shall support two-phase commit" algorithms, but there may be, for example, a commercial DDBMS that utilizes a different algorithm that would be automatically eliminated by the more restrictive version of the requirement.
4. As with the above, the appendix would illustrate examples of time- and change-oriented incremental backups.
5. In real life, each utility would be further explained in detail. To save, we have simply provided a list of functions.
6. The explicit mention of "any topology . . . " is noted if, for example, there is not an inherent prejudice towards a particular technology (Ethernet, token ring), protocol set (TCP/IP, ISO), or other characteristics. This statement is included only to free vendors to develop and propose the best possible solution without being unnecessarily constrained.
7. The referenced appendix would detail all of the applicable algorithms, which is important since there could be multiple definitions as to exactly what "just-in-time" inventory management is. (A tongue-in-cheek definition could be that the vendor completes the software "just in time" prior to the deadline.)
8. A full-scale RFP should also go into more detail regarding the reports, including sample output, lists of fields, or other guidance as to the contents of the report.
9. It would be appropriate in the LTD prototype appendix to include a list of guidelines for the prototype software, including acceptability of applications-generator-created systems, sample data, and other material.
10. At this point the RFP should discuss appropriate liquidated damages, which state's laws shall govern the contract terms, and other appropriate legal matters.

7

Writing
Winning
Proposals

Introduction

The proposal is one of the most important types of document you will
write during your career as a computer professional. This is no overstatement; regardless of whether you spend your entire career in large
corporations, on a consulting career, in academia, or another environment, you will find yourself depending on proposals to win approval for
projects and programs, obtain consulting or contract work, change an
educational curriculum or add areas of specialization to a degree program, or for many other important aspects of your career in the computer field.

There are many different characteristics and variations of proposals,
and this chapter discusses these major variables. We'll talk about the
purpose of proposals, how to align a proposal with your fundamental
strategy, how best to present your capabilities and qualifications, and
common mistakes to avoid. We'll look at two sample proposals, one
being a response to the RFP in Chap. 6, and the other an unsolicited internal proposal from an educational environment.

Proposal formats, contents, and other characteristics differ, sometimes radically, based on the characteristics and other factors discussed in this chapter. Therefore—and this is extremely important, so
we will repeat it several times in this chapter—*each proposal should be
treated as a unique entity that is prepared for a unique situation.* Extremely subtle distinctions, such as how you present your company's
capabilities in a particular situation, can often make the difference be-

tween success and failure in the proposal process. Again, we emphasize the importance of carefully examining each and every component of a proposal during preparation and revision.

The Purpose of Proposals

A proposal is a written statement of your (1) intention, (2) willingness, and (3) qualifications to accomplish a particular mission. Missions include:

- Developing a computer system
- Responding affirmatively to a *Request for Proposal* (RFP) and showing that you or your firm can accomplish the task
- Starting a project within your company or organization

A proposal provides a written *record* of your (1) intentions, (2) willingness, and (3) qualifications. *The very act of putting these three categories into writing signifies a commitment on your part above and beyond any verbal statements.* It is one thing, for example, to listen to someone describe a series of tasks that must be completed, and to respond with, "Yeah, we can do that." However, as with buying automobiles, real estate, investments, and other items, the absence of a *written* commitment to perform or provide some items at a specified price leaves too much room for misunderstanding and contention between the parties to a transaction. Not only is the recipient of the proposal protected by having a written record of specific commitments, *but you, the proposal writer, are also protected from claims that you committed yourself to perform a set of tasks that in actuality you didn't commit to do.* All in all, a written proposal forms the basis for written contracts of performance, so the more items in writing the better for all parties involved.

Proposals also function as *sales and marketing tools,* particularly in external situations. When submitting a proposal to another company or organization, you are giving that company a document which, if properly prepared, contains a great deal of information that is part of your sales and marketing strategy. Statements of qualifications and capabilities, references, presentations of creative or innovative solutions, and other components serve to tell the recipient that you *know* what you are doing, and in fact are *very good* at exactly what they would like you to do.

Proposals also serve as a *demonstration of your communications abilities,* both written (the document itself) and verbal (through follow-on briefings to and meetings with the recipient). While this may appear superficial, your professionalism and that of your organization are represented by your communications. In some cases, your proposal to a particular firm may be merely to work with them to prepare a proposal for another company (for example, to undertake a joint venture). In these cases, your demonstrated communications abilities may have a direct bearing on whether that firm will accept your proposal.

Proposals serve as a demonstration of your *organizational abilities*. Not only is the content being evaluated, but the recipients of your proposals are considering the manner in which it is presented. Intangibles such as the time frame in which a proposal is submitted (five seconds before the deadline? seven weeks after an informal request?) provide implicit statements as to your overall technical and professional capabilities.

For those readers who are primarily software coders with little or no experience with proposals, preparing a *good* proposal is analogous to the difference between developing software using structured techniques versus developing a GO TO-laden series of spaghetti programs. Both programs (or proposals) may work, but the more highly structured one reflects the ability to handle complex tasks better than the poorly structured one.

Finally, and perhaps most importantly, a proposal serves as the written extension of your *business or technical strategy*. It should be prepared *after* (or at least iteratively with) a situation-specific business or technical strategy, and should reflect that strategy in each and every sentence, paragraph, and page. Nothing is more confusing to someone who reads a proposal than inconsistencies in implicit messages, technical material, or other elements of a proposal. If your business strategy, for example, is to win a client's business at all costs in hopes of pursuing future work, your pricing strategy should reflect that goal. Similarly, if your technical strategy is to avoid risky, unproven technologies, be cautious about proposing products that are barely announced and may or may not be commercially available within your required time frame.

Characteristics of Proposals

Proposals may be solicited or unsolicited. Solicited proposals are often in response to *Requests for Proposals* (RFPs), a document form we discussed in the previous chapter. In other cases, a written proposal may be made in response to an informal request, as was done as the fictional conversation at the beginning of Chap. 6. Even in informal situations (discussed next), your proposal should be in writing for the reasons discussed earlier in this chapter.

Proposals may also be categorized as formal or informal. The primary distinctions between proposals that fall into one or the other of these categories are size and format.[1] Informal proposals tend to be shorter, often taking the form of a long business letter.[2] Many of the "overhead" components of proposals are reduced in length or even eliminated in informal proposals, given the likely familiarity of the parties involved with one another. For example, the section dealing with the proposal writer's capabilities and qualifications may be eliminated if one of the parties previously did work for the other.

As we mentioned earlier, proposals should be custom tailored for each and every situation. Assume that you are preparing proposals in response to two solicitations, one each from two different companies. One is for the installation of a *local area network* (LAN), along with custom development of a number of software systems that must interface to the LAN. The other is to develop a long-range strategic plan for a Fortune 500 company; the plan will include five-year pro forma cost analysis, a long-range migration plan for client/server technology, and staffing recommendations during the period under analysis.

Your statement of capabilities and qualifications should be written differently for each of these proposals. While both forms should include items such as how long your firm has been in business, and refer to a demonstrated record of success, the format for the LAN project should stress *hands-on* LAN experience and software development, listing many or all of the similar projects you have completed successfully. The other proposal, however, should stress your background in strategic planning and business-related issues, and list your references for similar types of projects and programs.

Marketing messages, proposal format, and all other elements should be similarly adapted to each and every situation.

Given that proposals represent you and your company or organization, their *appearance* is very important. As with business plans and other documents, the widespread use of laser printers and graphical software provides even individuals with the capability to produce attractive, professional documents. Graphics, charts, and tables should be used in conjunction with the text. A caution: There is sometimes a tendency to over-use fonts, text sizes, textual attributes such as shadowing and outlining, and other capabilities available with modern document preparation tools; these should be used intelligently, but rapid changes in fonts and other elements actually can detract from your proposal. Be careful not to over-use such capabilities.

Proposal *size* should be determined by the situation. If your proposal is in response to a request for prices for specific software packages and some simple installation work, it should be shorter than one detailing highly complex software development tasks. Many RFPs specify a maximum length for responding proposals; these specifications should not be violated.

Internal versus External Proposals

Proposals may also be categorized by whether they are submitted within your organization (internal) or to another company or organization (external). It is very important to realize that internal proposals are not always informal, nor are external proposals always formal (see Fig. 7.1). For example, a proposal submitted to another company for whom you have done many projects may be rather informal, while an internal proposal for a major program, directed to a vice president whom you have never met, may be more formal. As we mentioned before, the format of each proposal should be considered individually.

Alternative Solutions

Several years ago, one of the authors of this book was working with a government consulting firm that was putting together a proposal in response to an Air Force solicitation for an office information system and local area network. Among the hardware portions of the system were various peripherals, including laser printers and *optical character readers* (OCRs). Our firm responded to the specified numbers of high-speed and low-speed laser printers and OCRs, but also attached an appendix to our proposal showing how the Air Force agency could utilize alternative printer and OCR configurations that would provide the required system-wide throughput (printed pages per minute for the printers, scanned pages per minute for the OCRs), yet save almost $1 million! Naturally, we assumed that the Air Force's procurement

	Formal	Informal
Internal	Proposal to fund and begin major product development effort	Proposal to your immediate manager to approve additional staffing for a small-scale project
External	Response to a government RFP	Letter to your long-time client suggesting that he/she upgrade his/her hardware and software environment

Figure 7.1 Matrix of proposal categories.

agency would gladly and gratefully accept our proposed changes and weigh them heavily in our favor for the contract award.

We were surprised, then, when at our first face-to-face meeting with the government's procurement team we were told to remove the entire appendix in which we proposed our configuration changes, or we would be immediately disqualified from the competition for the contract. As we learned, many government agencies aren't the least bit concerned with saving money on proposed contracts if it requires extensive amounts of paperwork to modify their RFPs once they have been released for competition. Therefore, always try to get a feel for the particular people and agencies with whom you are dealing before you propose alternative solutions to a formal RFP in your proposal; your good intentions may actually result in problems.

Capabilities and Qualifications

The statement of capabilities and qualifications within your proposal is a very important part of it, and can often have either a positive or negative influence on a decision to award a contract to you. We mentioned earlier that statements of capabilities should be tailored to each and every situation, depending on the primary needs and concerns of the person or organization for whom the proposal is intended. Capabilities statements should include:

1. *The qualifications of the company or organization on whose behalf the proposal is being submitted.* This is true for internal as well as external proposals, since in many internal situations multiple organizations are competing for dollars and resources, and sometimes directly against one another for a specific program.

2. *The qualifications of key individuals.* This is particularly crucial for proposals submitted on behalf of individuals (that is, your own consulting company) or small firms, but is important for any proposal. For example, if your organization is submitting a proposal to a company vice president to develop an integrated CASE platform for commercial resale (and, therefore, requesting a budget of several million dollars), it is important to emphasize the accomplishments and successes of key individuals of your team *in this technology and related technical areas.* The capabilities should be presented in a manner similar to that of a business plan (see sample at end of Chap. 8).

3. *Past experience that may be relative.* If your company is relatively new, but is made up of many people who left another firm to begin their own, related experience and successes at the former company may rightfully be referenced to highlight your organization's qualifications.

4. *Experience in industry leadership.* For example, if your firm can rightfully claim to be "the company that has installed and supported more of XYZ's software package than any other in the western United States," this should be emphasized in your statement of capabilities.

5. *Any statements that may provide a competitive advantage.* Assume that you are submitting a proposal to a company whose last contracting experience resulted in the vendor going far over budget and charging excessively for the overages (a common occurrence in government contracting, as we all know). A statement in your qualifications section that reads something like, "ABC Company has always welcomed fixed price contracts, and has never, in twelve years of operations, delivered a client's system late," may give the recipient of your proposal more confidence in you.

6. *Company financials, if applicable.* In some situations—particularly large, multiyear programs—the recipient of your proposal may want assurance that your firm is stable and is likely to remain in business, particularly in difficult times such as the early 1990s. Inclusion of your company's financials, particularly if you have a strong balance sheet and can show an excellent record of growth, can be an important part of your statement of qualifications.

7. *Education and training background.* Somewhat related to individuals' capabilities, there are situations where professional degrees and training (product-specific, technology oriented, and so on) can be important. For example, if you are just beginning a career in the computer field and are attempting to do full-time or part-time consulting but have little or no track record of working world accomplishments, you may be able to convince a client to award a project to you, based on your education and training.

8. *References to formal "company capabilities" documents.* Some consulting companies have a formal "company capabilities" document that contains an exhaustive review of a company's history, financial picture, references, and other information. This document may provide the basis for the situation-specific statements of qualifications that can be adapted to individual proposals. Where applicable, references to the "overall capabilities" document should be included in the proposal.

Formats of Proposals

As with most of the other documents we discuss in this book, the *formats* of proposals should be adapted to individual situations. One recommended format, as discussed in *The Consultant's Guide to Proposal Writing* by Herman Holtz,[3] is discussed below.

Section I: Introduction

1. *About the offerer.* An introductory portion that provides some lead-in to Section IV.

2. *Understanding of the requirement.* This portion is intended to demonstrate that you have a clear understanding of the prospective client's needs and opportunities.

Section II: Discussion

1. *The requirement.* This portion expands the previous subsection into a detailed explanation of the requirements. Together with the next two portions, this section would, for example, form the bulk of the technical response to an RFP or comprise the technical marketing presentation for an unsolicited proposal.

2. *Analysis.* This subsection describes your analysis of the client's environment.

3. *Approach.* This is where you tell *how* you will satisfy the requirements at hand.

Section III: Proposed Project

The subsections of this section detail a number of project-specific organizational, staffing, and procedural management items with respect to the project. These include:

1. Project organization
2. Management
3. Plans and procedures
4. Staff
5. Deliverable items
6. Schedules
7. Resume(s)

Section IV: Qualifications and Experience

1. *Relevant current and recent projects.* This is the situationally adaptable portion about which we wrote earlier; the most relevant successes of you or your organization should be emphasized here.

2. *Resources.* All of your available resources, including employees, subcontract assistance, development environments, and so on, should be detailed here.

Miscellaneous

Front matter. An attractive title page and other introductory material

Appendices. As necessary

Cautions

As important as what to include in a proposal and how it is presented
are what *not* to include and what *not* to do with respect to the proposal
process. Some of the things to avoid are:[4]

1. *An aggressive or defensive posture.* Especially in these highly competitive times, it is not wise to prepare a proposal that has an underlying tone of aggressiveness; that is, "Hey, Mr. or Ms. Client or
   Vice President, here is what I will do, under my terms, and here is
   what you will pay for the privilege of having me do this for you."
   Anyone who follows the business and general news of late has seen
   that attorneys, consultants, accountants, and other professionals
   are now having to scale back their aggressive stances that were
   prevalent during the 1980s.

2. *A "loud-claims" proposal.* Clients and internal decision-makers
   evaluate proposals based on substance, not merely claims of superiority or promises to accomplish some tasks.

3. *A proposal that does not distinguish you from the rest of the crowd.*
   Your proposal should show why you can perform the required tasks
   better than your competition, not merely as well as they can.

4. *A proposal that indicates an uncertainty as to the client's requirements.* This tactic is used when a proposal writer figures that "you,
   the client, should tell me what you want to do and I will do it; we'll
   get to the details later." Managers and clients want some degree of
   comfort that the selected recipient of a project knows the details as
   well as or better than they do.

5. *A canned solution.* Earlier we spoke about ensuring that proposals
   are adapted according to each situation. A dangerous tactic is to
   present a solution that "worked last time for another client with
   similar needs" without investigating new products, technologies,
   prices, and other aspects of a solution.

Discussing Your Competition

The manner in which you discuss your competition in the body of a proposal is very important. As we mentioned in the previous section, you
want to tell the client why you, and you alone, are the best person or

company or organization to complete a task, start a project, or otherwise successfully complete what is covered in your proposal. Only in rare situations will you be the sole competitor for a contract, or the only organization within a corporation fighting to begin a major new program or project.

Sometimes your competition is not known to you; in many cases, however, you do have some idea of who your competition is. Just as many people are turned off by negative political advertising and, if only in protest, vote against the perpetrator of such a campaign, so too are many recipients of proposals alienated by overt claims of superiority over specific competitors when those claims are denigrating to the competition.

You might refer to your competition in this manner: "Our firm has a greater aggregate amount of LAN experience than any other consulting firm in the Rocky Mountain area." A claim such as this one, with passive references to the competition in direct comparison to your own capabilities, shows a high degree of professionalism in your choice of words. In contrast, a statement such as: "Our competition, particularly XYZ Company, has a terrible reputation for missing deadlines and consistently overcharging their unfortunate customers" should be avoided. While it may be true, you would open yourself and your company to legal action, and would risk alienating the prospective client ("If they say this about their competition, do they likewise badmouth their customers?" might be a client's thought).

Summary

Of all the document types we discuss in this book, proposals may have the most permutations of form and content. A number of factors—solicited or unsolicited, formal or informal, internal or external—influence how proposals will be created and presented.

End Notes

1. Herman Holtz, *The Consultant's Guide to Proposal Writing*, Wiley, New York, 1986.
2. Ibid.
3. Ibid., pp. 13–17.
4. Ibid., pp. 22–23.

Two Sample Proposals

Since proposals can vary so widely in their format and content, we have included two samples in this chapter. The first is a response to the RFP from the previous chapter, and the second is a representative internal proposal from a development manager to a corporate vice president; the purpose of this proposal is to start up an ambitious internal development program.

JSAS Consulting, Inc.

Proposal to Michaelson Electronics, Inc.

Response to RFP #1215

Office Information System

February 14, 1992

Submitted by:

JSAS Consulting, Inc.
8111 Grant Blvd.
Tucson, AZ 85000

To:

Michaelson Electronics, Inc.
1212 Waterbridge Avenue
Phoenix, AZ 85200

Table of Contents

Introduction

About JSAS Consulting

The Michaelson Electronics Office Information System

Response to RFP Requirements

Introduction

Word Processing

Distributed Database Management System (DDBMS)

Graphics Software and Presentation System

System Administration and Network Management

Local Area Network (LAN) Environment

Inventory Management Applications Software

The JSAS Consulting Approach

Project Organization

Management

Plans and Procedures

Staff

Deliverable Items

Schedules

Resumes of Key Personnel

JSAS Consulting Capabilities and Qualifications

Introduction

About JSAS Consulting

JSAS Consulting has served the computer consulting needs of small businesses across Arizona and the mountain states since 1982. JSAS Consulting specializes in distributed information systems solutions, and has extensive experience in all LAN topologies and architectures.

JSAS Consulting has extensive experience in office information systems, including those similar to that required by Michaelson Electronics. The firm's specific experience is detailed later in this proposal.

The Michaelson Electronics Office Information System (OIS)

The solution presented in this proposal will provide Michaelson Electronics with state of the art, expandable OIS capabilities. The distributed database management system proposed by JSAS Consulting is closely integrated not only with the inventory management software but with the word processing and graphics packages as well; both software systems can extract distributed database-resident information and (1) include the resulting information in word processing documents, as well as (2) present the information in graphical format, both in document form and through slideshow presentation facilities.

It is very important to manage distributed information systems resources consistently, and the JSAS network management solution provides CMIP (common management information protocol) support for distributed resource management.

Response to RFP Requirements

Introduction

All software proposed by JSAS Consulting as part of this proposal conforms to the required microcomputer platform specification as presented in RFP #1215. Specifically, the following configuration alternatives are available for any Michaelson Electronics microcomputer:

- MS-DOS 3.31, 4.0, or 5.0
- 80386 or 80486 processor
- Clock speed of 16 MHz or faster
- Hard disk of 80 Mb or greater capacity
- A minimum 1.5 Mb of main memory
- LookAtMe V2.5 window and task management software, operating in expanded memory mode

The sections that follow detail the JSAS Consulting solution for each of the technical areas.[1]

Word processing

JSAS Consulting has selected WritingRight V4.0 as the best commercially available word processing package for the Michaelson Electronics OIS. As detailed below, all Michaelson Electronics word processing requirements as stated in RFP #1215 are supported by WritingRight V4.0.

a   Simultaneous use and availability.   Each user shall be able to invoke WritingRight V4.0 at any time his or her desktop computer is available. WritingRight V4.0 runs on each local desktop system, with access to network-based file servers limited to document access. No user is impacted by any network downtime.

b   Windowed environment.   WritingRight V4.0 operates in multitasking mode under LookAtMe V2.5 window and task management software. Each user can have up to 20 windows open, exclusive of header, footer, and spelling windows. Documents may be split between two or more windows at user discretion. Context switches to another word processing window are accomplished in a maximum of 0.2 seconds.

c Presentation capabilities. WritingRight V4.0 supports the following:

(1) Inclusion of editable graphics from PrettyPicture V2.0, the graphics package proposed by JSAS Consulting. The included graphics images scroll together with text, and PrettyPicture V2.0 can be invoked directly from WritingRight V4.0, as well as under the LookAtMe V2.5 multitasking environment.

(2) Screen presentation of the following fonts and textual attributes, as derived directly from WritingRight V4.0 (this document was prepared in WritingRight V4.0):

Fonts

Times

Helvetica

Bookman

Palatino

Text sizes

9 point

10 point

12 point

14 point

18 point

24 point

Textual attributes

Solid underline

Word-only underline

Double underline

~~Strike-through~~

Boldface

Italics

d Document size. WritingRight V4.0 is capable of editing a document up to 2 gigabytes in size through its *virtual document facility* (VDF). No user action is required for document segment management.

e Subwindows. Each WritingRight V4.0 window shall be capable of being split into three subwindows. Subwindow access is accomplished by a single mouseclick action, and maximum context switching time is 0.005 seconds.

f Spelling verification. WritingRight V4.0 contains a built-in spelling dictionary of 125,000 words. Each user can create up to 10 personal dictionaries. The built-in and personal dictionaries are both consulted by the word processing spelling verification system without the user having to specifically request which dictionary shall be consulted. The spelling verification system has a "suggest correct word" mode where likely candidates to replace an incorrect word are presented to the user for selection. The spelling verification system will, at user option, ignore words with all capital letters.

g Physical document size. WritingRight V4.0 supports physical document sizes up to 40″ wide.

h Margins. Left and right margins shall be selectable in either inches or centimeters in WritingRight V4.0.

i Tabs. Users can place an unlimited number of left, right, center, and decimal tabs at any point in a document, and change the settings on each and every line.

Distributed database management

JSAS Consulting has proposed DataDisperse V1.0 as the distributed DBMS product for the Michaelson Electronics OIS. DataDisperse V1.0 is the recognized leader in heterogeneous DBMS access and management, and is SQL Access compliant for subsequent client/server DDBMS capabilities at Michaelson Electronics. The individual requirements of RFP #1215 are addressed below.

a Remote access. Any DataDisperse V1.0 user can retrieve data from a remote node without having to perform any node specification functions.

b Distributed partitions. DataDisperse V1.0 supports both horizontal and vertical partitions. The DataDisperse V1.0 *data definition language* (DDL) permits seven different manners of partitioning parameters to be specified. All global operations are performed by the DBMS without user action.

c Distributed concurrency control. DataDisperse V1.0 supports distributed concurrency control and distributed locking algorithms through a two-phase commit protocol. The distributed locking algorithms support both time-out and deadlock resolution mechanisms.

d Rollback. DataDisperse V1.0 supports distributed rollback of any transaction in progress to the state prior to the beginning of the transaction, whether by user or application request or through deadlock resolution. All data and metadata at all nodes are restored to their state at the time prior to the beginning of the transaction following a rollback. No other simultaneous transactions are affected by the rollback.

e Metadata management. All DataDisperse V1.0 metadata definitions are stored in an IRDS-compliant centralized repository.

f Language. The DataDisperse V1.0 language supports all features of the SQL-92 standard, Level 2.

g Distributed security. The DDBMS supports two levels of security:

(1) Authorization of users through the SQL-92 GRANT and REVOKE statements.
(2) Authentication of remote nodes through a patented algorithm that has been verified by U.S. Government communications securities agencies.

Graphics and presentation software

PrettyPicture V2.0 is the graphics and presentation software package selected by JSAS Consulting to best meet the requirements of the Michaelson Electronics RFP. PrettyPicture V2.0 was selected as "Software Product of the Year" for 1991 by *PC Software World* magazine, just as V1.0 of the product was given the same honor in 1989.

a Supported graphics. PrettyPicture V2.0 automatically creates the following types of graphs from selected input data:

- Horizontal bar
- Vertical bar
- Pie
- Broken pie
- Line
- Column

b Annotations. Users of PrettyPicture V2.0 can specify and modify annotations on any graphical data item, along with the vertical and horizontal axis titles, legends, and chart titles.

c Data input. PrettyPicture V2.0 can accept input from CalcVille spreadsheets, DataDisperse V1.0, and from direct input into a spreadsheetlike template. The input data can be included under the LookAtMe V2.5 heterogeneous cut and paste facility.

d Colors. Users can select from a palette of 512 colors. Any individual item within the graphics software—data items, annotations, shadings, horizontal axis, vertical axis—can be capable of individual selection of its color from the palate.

e Slide show capabilities. Users can create and play a "slide show" of PrettyPicture V2.0 graphics screens. The slide show permits forward and backward scrolling, adjustable time intervals for automatic scrolling, and automatic modification of slide ordering within the package itself; no external software is required.

Inventory management system[2]

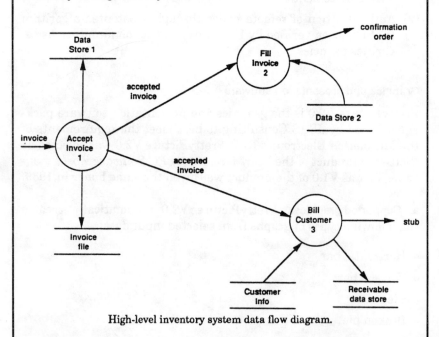

High-level inventory system data flow diagram.

The JSAS Consulting Approach[3]

Project organization

JSAS Consulting utilizes a unique, highly successful project management technique. A matrix management approach is utilized where the line program manager and his or her direct subordinates are supported by the "mentor staff," a team of technical experts that assist individual developers and team leaders with technical issue resolution. This approach will work extremely well during the development of the Michaelson Electronics OIS, since the mentor staff contains experts in distributed database management systems as well as desktop software integration. Additionally, a senior vice president is assigned direct responsibility for ensuring the success of the program. The mentor staff and the vice presidential sponsor aid the process of vendor interface and other issues, letting the program manager focus on operational issues and client interfaces.

Ms. Ann Meadows (her biography is presented later) has been selected as the program manager. She will have direct control over all resources assigned to the OIS.

Schedules

The following schedule is proposed for the Michaelson Electronics OIS:

September 1, 1992: Begin OIS program

September 1–October 5, 1992: Word processing and graphics software installation

October 5–October 31, 1992: User word processing and graphics software training

October 12–November 15, 1992: Installation of DDBMS software

September 15–October 30, 1992: Specification and design period for inventory management system

October 30, 1992: Design review for inventory management system

October 31, 1992–February 15, 1993: Development of inventory management system

JSAS Consulting Capabilities and Qualifications

JSAS Consulting has served the computer consulting needs of small businesses across Arizona and the mountain states since 1982. JSAS Consulting has installed, developed, or managed over 300 LAN-based environments among its client base, more than any other firm in the four corners states.

The firm was founded in 1982 by Richard Fiddler, and has grown from a two-person company to a staff of 125 highly qualified computer professionals. Graduates from the leading computer science and business information systems programs—MIT, Stanford, and Georgia Tech, to name a few—have joined JSAS Consulting.

JSAS Consulting has successfully developed over 45 office information system environments, several of which are nearly identical in function to that requested by Michaelson Electronics. These include:

- *American Cola Distributors, Phoenix.* A 750-station PC network environment with word processing, spreadsheet, and graphics capabilities built on top of a distributed DBMS platform.

- *National Filmmaker Institute, Tucson.* A 350-station PC network with distributed database server capabilities and a custom-developed inventory management system.

- *Consolidated Fishing of Arizona, Phoenix.* A PC network that began with 75 users and has grown to 2000 stations. A custom-developed inventory management system interfaces with commercial accounting software.

Proposal End Notes

1. In the interest of space, we have included responses to only some sections of the sample RFP (just as the sample RFP contains only a limited number of entries for each technical area). A real-life response would address each and every RFP technical item.
2. We have included only sample graphics; this section would be likely to have graphics because custom software development is required.
3. As with the above section, we have included representative portions of this section.

Wadsworth Software Inc.

Proposal:
Integrated CASE Product
Development

February 15, 1992

Michael Evanworth
Software Tools Development Manager,
Languages and Tools
(210) 555-8888

Distribution and Approval List

Walter Moriarty, Senior Development Manager

Cathy Burrows, Director of New Products

Merle Palmer, Vice President of Products and Operations

Related Documents:
Wadsworth Software Strategic Directions, 12/91
Wadsworth Software Marketing Strategy, 10/91

Executive Summary

The Software Tools (ST) organization is proposing that Wadsworth Software bring an integrated CASE (I-CASE) platform to market in Q2 1994. ST has completed two successful prototypes of an integration platform, both of which have been demonstrated to senior Wadsworth executives as well as selected strategic customer partners.

The program will provide an internal rate of return of 47% over a seven-year product life cycle. Enhanced, upwardly compatible versions of the product are scheduled at 12-month intervals over the product life cycle.

The I-CASE platform will establish Wadsworth Software as an industry leader in the CASE marketplace, and through the nature of the platform will further cement strategic relationships with leading software vendors in the CASE, repository, and database markets.

The Integrated CASE Marketplace and Opportunities for Wadsworth Software[1]

Development Schedule[2]

The following development schedule is under way for the Wadsworth Software I-CASE platform, based on approval of R&D funds in 1990.

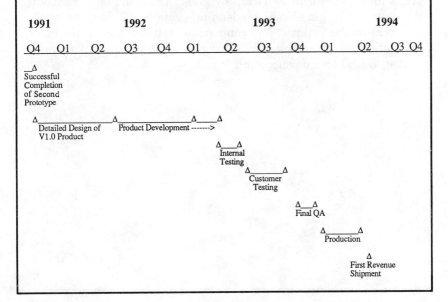

Financial Plans

(This section would contain financial plans similar to those found in the sample business plan in Chap. 8, with a breakdown of development costs and projected revenues.)

The Software Tools Organization[3]

The Software Tools organization of Wadsworth Software was formed in 1984. Since that time, ST has an unbroken record of developing commercially successful, technologically superior products that have been critically acclaimed. These include the following:

Product	First shipment	Direct product revenue	Service revenue	IRR
DesignDataStore	1986	$2.3M	$1.8M	42%
FlowDraw	1987	$3.1M	$1.9M	52%
SwitchPage	1987	$1.9M	$1.2M	41%
PlaneDraw	1989	$4.2M	$2.8M	68%
FilmStore	1990	$3.8M	$0.8M	55%
FrameSwapper	1991	$0.7M	$0.7M	31%

The ST organization has steadily brought talented software developers into Wadsworth Software by giving them the opportunity to work on challenging, industry-leading projects. ST has one of the lowest turnover ratios of any comparable software development organization in the industry, resulting in a high degree of stability among Wadsworth development teams.

Proposal End Notes

1. This section would contain an analysis similar to that of the sample business plan contained in Chap. 8 where the marketplace and competition are analyzed and evaluated.
2. When possible, include milestones to date in the proposal (example: completion of prior prototypes) to lend credibility to the suggestion that approval of the proposal constitutes a logical next step in an ongoing process.
3. On many occasions, an internal organization is fighting not only for approval of funds, but also competing against other organizations for the specific project. It is advisable to include the equivalent of a "capabilities and qualifications" statement in internal proposals, especially when sending proposals to vice presidents of large companies, who may not even be familiar with your organization or the key personnel involved.

Chapter

8

Business Plans

Computer professionals often think the time and effort necessary to prepare a business plan is time that could be spent doing other meaningful tasks. After all, you know what your product or service will do in the market—or do you? Why do you need to let others know? The reason is that business plans are an essential element in your success as a computer professional. They are a part of the communication relationship you are attempting to establish, discussed in Chap. 12. Coupled with business letters, discussed in Chap. 11, business plans establish the written communication portion of the communication relationship. They provide constructive notice to the world of your intentions and plans. While communicating your business plans to others outside your organization is beneficial, often the notice it provides to those within your organization is the real benefit.

The business plan is a written organizational vehicle for communicating the strategic map of how you will achieve your goals. A business plan forces you to think about all aspects of your venture, some of which you might otherwise overlook if you were not writing the business plan.

If you are interested in consulting, it is easy to view yourself as an independent contractor progressing from one engagement to another. There may come a time, however, when you will have to provide your client with a business plan as part of your consulting function. Even if you are not operating your own business, you, as a computer professional, may be asked to write business plans for use internally within a large organization. In fact, it is increasingly standard business practice that the approval of funding is based upon the demonstration of a viable business plan. Your business plan's viability is directly related to the skills, including communication skills, you have invested in it.

Business Plan Components

The first step in preparing a business plan is a feasibility study, discussed in Chap. 4. This study shows whether or not the business plan is viable. Once the feasibility study shows that a market exists, you need to proceed with an outline of your business plan. As with all business operations, each business plan must relate to the particular situation. Accordingly, the level of detail provided in the business plan depends on the nature of the plan itself. There are, however, some basic components that should at least be examined in every business plan[1]:

- Summary: An executive overview
- The concept
- The market
- Competition
- The organization
- Your credentials
- The product or service
- Production plans
- Pricing
- The marketing plan
- The financial plan
- Time schedule
- Operating systems
- Control systems
- Growth plans
- Contingency plans
- The deal

We will briefly examine these components of the business plan, and in specific sections, where applicable, discuss the role communication plays.

Summary: An executive overview

The summary, or executive overview, is the first part of the business plan, and gives the highlights of your plan. This overview is intended to answer some basic questions: What you will do, how you will do it, and what is needed to accomplish the task. You should direct the responses to these questions to the intended audience, as discussed under "Audience Reference" in Chap. 13. This is also the opportunity to include a brief statement of the actions your reader must perform; the detailed request for action should be included in the last section of the business plan. The most important feature of this business plan component is the means of gaining the attention and interest of your reader. Remember, this is the beginning of a communication relationship. For it to proceed to the next stage, you must gain the reader's interest.

The concept

The concept is the cog in the wheel of your business plan. It is the reason the plan exists. Your ability to clearly and precisely communicate the concept is essential to your reader's understanding of the overall business plan. It may be beneficial to create a conceptual model[2] to precisely answer the following questions:

- What value is to be exchanged
- To whom
- For what
- By what means
- Where
- Made by whom
- Marketed by whom
- Financed by whom

The key to this section is your ability to communicate your concept. This will enable you to lay the foundation for a conceptually effective business plan.

The market

Your concept is intended to fill an existing gap in the marketplace. In this section of your business plan your job is convincing the reader that a market exists for your service or product. Any and all relevant marketing data should be used as backup support. This section must answer decisively any doubts that the reader has concerning market demand. As briefly discussed in Chap. 1 and thoroughly examined in Chap. 13, "satisfaction" is a presentation strategy that can also be used in business plans. Satisfaction is your ability to answer any questions or doubts your reader may have before they become real, concrete concerns. After reviewing this section of your business plan, your reader should believe, if only in concept, that a market exists for your product or service.

Competition

Many people like to view competition as being nonexistent because they believe the service or product they will provide is unique. In reality, most concepts are not totally original, and thus competition does exist. Knowing (through personal examination) who your competition is will give you new insight into your own concept. Examine and compare its strengths and weaknesses, and at the same time, try to differentiate your concept from your competition's and show why your implementation of the concept is better.

Additionally, your business plan should review all competition, including existing competitors and those you believe currently are working on a similar concept. Your examination should also include those competitors that in the recent past have divested themselves of a competing concept. This is important, because if you need to obtain financing, your financing sources may needlessly be concerned that competition exists when actually it does not.

The organization/Your credentials

These sections answer the basic "who" question. If you are a consultant, the answer to this "who" question often is "me, myself, and I." Even if you are working for a large organization, often you will find yourself in the lead role in developing a concept. Therefore it is imperative that you "sell" yourself in these sections. No matter how creative or unique your concept, if you can not convince others that you have the ability to execute the business plan, nothing will happen. Credibility, discussed in Chap. 1 and explored in Chap. 13 as a speech skill, is also an essential element in written communication. You should communicate that you have the credentials and the credibility necessary to implement your business plan. Remember, your business plan is selling more than a concept; it is selling your skills.

The product or service

This section of the business plan should give your reader an overview of the product or service. It is especially easy for computer technicians to fall into the trap of providing too much detailed, technical information. Most technical information should be provided in a separate presentation after the business plan has been reviewed. Therefore you need to provide a sufficient amount of basic information to be informative without overloading the reader with technical details. It is important in this section to know the correct amount of information to provide to maximize the effectiveness of your communication.

Production plans

If your business plan involves a product, this is your opportunity to answer the "made by whom" question in the "Concept" section. Even as a consultant offering a service rather than a product, this section forces you to examine the costs and timing of your services, detailed in the "Pricing" and "Time schedule" sections, respectively.

Pricing

Remember those economics classes where the intersection of supply and demand curves determined the equilibrium prices? They're back! Actually, we bring to mind these economic graphs only to illustrate the point that it is often difficult to price a new concept. After all, pricing is a function of supply and demand curves, which are determined by external forces. You need to price your concept realistically. A good starting point for pricing is comparing your concept to other existing and similar products or services. What will the market bear for your concept? This section of the business plan sometimes may include a financial analysis, including a break-even analysis.

The marketing plan

Marketing is often viewed as the "touchy, feely" discipline in business. However, marketing is the key to your product's success. The marketing plan should include defining and segmenting the market; this answers the "marketing by whom" portion of the conceptual model discussed in the "Concept" section of your business plan. Once you have defined your market, you need to explore marketing strategies: How will you get your product or service message to your target market?

There are a myriad of marketing angles for your concept. You must keep in mind, however, that marketing plans are to some degree based on underlying current marketing trends that mirror the general economic mood. Accordingly, marketing to your computer market probably should involve the concept of value, because ". . . value is becoming the marketer's watchword for the 1990s."[3] Value comprises realistic pricing, service, and quality.

A word of caution: Spend an ample amount of time on the marketing plan. This section of your business plan requires proactive and creative thinking on your part because you have already made the assumption that your concept is viable in the market; now you need to focus on how to convince your reader that it is salable.

The financial plan

The financial portion of your business plan should provide concrete evidence that your concept is feasible financially. After all, the world's most innovative concept will remain only a concept unless it is financially sound. This section of your business plan serves as an internal double check because it forces you to think of your concept purely in financial terms, which in turn provides an important component to the macro question of your concept's viability.

The hallmark of financing for the 1990s is summed up in a brief sentence: It is difficult to obtain. The capital available for financing new ventures has become increasingly competitive because of the general economic climate. Therefore, it is vital that you provide an accurate and complete financial analysis so that the reader, who may be a venture capitalist, feels confident that the concept is viable. If your business plan is internal within a large organization, funding is predicated to a great extent on the business plan's financial analysis.

Your financial analysis should include a balance sheet (see sample business plan at the end of this chapter). Once your concept has become an active, real entity, the income statement will enable you to focus on the current operations level, with the balance sheet being of secondary importance. Conversely, in the start-up phase, including the business plan, the balance sheet is the most vital piece of financial information you can provide. Venture capitalists, bankers, and other money sources have general guidelines to follow, and the balance sheet provides the essential elements of financial information.

Cash flow is used increasingly as a tool to examine financial strength. The 1980s debt hangover has resulted in the reexamination of the importance of cash flow in the success or failure of a business. The cash flow statement (see sample business plan at the end of this chapter) combines your balance sheet and income statement to become a forecasting tool for your concept.

Time schedule

The old adage that "time is money" holds true for your concept; time can be viewed as a constraint. Consequently, you need to provide a realistic assessment of the time required to bring to the market your product or service. This timetable should include all phases of your concept, from inception to production to market introduction. If other individuals or companies are a necessary part of your concept, be sure to have them provide you with their timing estimates. Your goal in this section of your business plan is to have your timeframe as accurate as possible. As we will discuss under the "Contingency plan" portion of your business plan, allow yourself some extra contingency time. Murphy's Law, unfortunately, is often applicable with a new concept.

Operating systems/Control systems

At this point in your business plan, hopefully you have convinced the reader that the various aspects of your concept, including the marketing and financial plans, are doable. Your task, however, has only begun. A quick look at the real estate industry will confirm the importance of this section of your business plan. Commercial real estate developers, especially in the early 1980s, easily found financial backing for their projects, with each new development analogous to a concept in a business plan. The key component not examined, however, was the long-term viability of the project once the up-front fees had been taken by all the interested parties. Consequently, asset management, better defined as the ability to operate and control the project, became the key to the success or failure of most commercial real estate projects in the 1990s.

The bottom line: Once you have your concept, can you operate and manage it within the control systems you have designated. Your ability to provide your reader with a comfort level for ongoing operations is an essential part of your business plan. Included within this section should be an operating budget (see example at the end of chapter) which will provide key future financial information to the reader and serve as supplementary information to the financial plan you provide.

Growth plans

Growth plans provide the business plan reader with insight into your future plans. An additional benefit of this section is the internal thought process it requires of you. Most of your time and effort in your business plan is concentrated on forecasting; you are required to make assumptions throughout the business plan about future events, and you should attempt to explain your assumptions as thoroughly as possible. Growth plans take you one step further, because they require you to think beyond the initial forecasting; you are required to project into the future, with the assumption that most things will go as planned. There will be snags along the way, so you must carefully analyze your concept under a variety of "what if" scenarios. These scenarios will provide you with your growth plans.

Contingency plans

This is another section of the business plan where the derived benefit is shared equally by you and the reader. Robert Burns' quotation that "the best laid schemes o' mice and men gang aft a-gley,"[4] anglicized to the familiar, "the best laid plans of mice and man are apt to go astray," rings as true about business as it does about life. Some things will not happen as planned, whether you have control over the events or not. Accordingly, you must have contingency plans to fall back on. Your ability to relate your plans briefly, without calling attention to potential problems, will show the reader that you have carefully examined them and planned for unexpected events. Thus this section shows your commitment and diligence in examining all facets of your concept.

The deal

As in all forms of written communication, it is important that you clearly state what you want of your readers if their action is required. In your business plan, most likely, this would involve the request for capital. You must be careful, however, not to specify in too much detail the ownership percentage you are willing to offer, because you do not want to lock yourself into a deal with specific terms. If a more beneficial deal comes along, you want to reserve the freedom to negotiate without the problem of having already promised a piece of the concept to another party. At the same time, if you want action on the part of your reader that does not involve a financial commitment, leave no doubt in the reader's mind about what you want.

Summary

The required analysis of the aforementioned components of your business plan will result in a professional communication tool to aid you in establishing your communication relationship. Your goals concerning your business plan readers are three Cs: communication, comprehension, and concurrence.

End Notes

1. Richard H. Buskirk, *The Entrepreneur's Handbook*, revised ed., Robert Brian Inc., Los Angeles, 1985, pp. 48–52.
2. Ibid., p. 134.
3. "Value Marketing," *Business Week*, November 11, 1991, p. 132.
4. John G. Bartlett, *Bartlett's Familiar Quotations*, 15th and 125th Anniversary Edition, Little, Brown, Boston, 1980.

Sample Business Plan

The AllCASE, Inc. business plan that follows is intended to provide you with an example of a plan utilizing the various components this chapter explored. Due to space limitations, not all components of the business plan we have discussed are presented. Additionally, please note that the information contained in this sample business plan is fictionalized data.

AllCASE, Inc.

Business Plan

February 1992

AllCASE, Inc.
9999 Speedway Blvd.
Tucson, AZ 85700
(602) 555-5858

Table of Contents[1]

Executive Summary

AllCASE, Inc. is a two-year-old company located in Tucson, Arizona. The company was founded in 1990 to exploit tremendous opportunities in the *integrated computer-aided software engineering* (I-CASE) marketplace. Although CASE technology has been available since the early 1980s, it has been slow to gain large-scale industry usage, primarily due to the lack of integration capabilities. The few integration efforts to date were provided by individual vendors with limited integration capabilities among their own tool offerings. *There have been no successful commercial CASE integration environments under which tools from multiple vendors can operate with one another.*

AllCASE, Inc. currently is developing its flagship product, the All-CASE Integration Framework. The product is scheduled for completion and availability in November 1993. As noted below and later in this business plan, the AllCASE Integration Framework's leadership position in the marketplace will lead to rapid profitability and tremendous returns on investment (ROI) for investors.

Fiscal Year Ending December 31

	1991	1992	1993	1994	1995
Revenue	124	145	224	21,400	35,700
Pretax profit/(loss)	(879)	(1,432)	(1,750)	2,350	12,750

All numbers in ($000s).

The Market

CASE

Computer-aided software engineering (CASE) is the process of using computer tools to assist the software development process. CASE methodologies have evolved from the structured programming movements of the 1970s, and products began to appear in the early 1980s. Most CASE tools utilize structured design methodologies and models, including entity-relationship diagrams, data-flow diagrams, structure charts, context diagrams, and other graphical tools.

CASE is extremely important to overcoming the growing software development backlog that has clogged the development pipelines for years. When tools and techniques are properly employed, the productivity gains from CASE have been demonstrated to be two to three times that of traditional, manual-oriented software development.

Integrated CASE

One of the shortcomings of CASE to date has been the lack of integration among the various components. CASE tools operate at all levels of the software development life cycle, from requirements collection to reverse engineering (see figure).

The integration problem arises when an organization attempts to use the output from one set of tools at a given life cycle stage as input to the next stage. Unless the tools are from the same vendor, and have been designed to work with one another, any data sharing must be accomplished through the cumbersome and inefficient process of reentering all data into the new tool.

Requirements	Specifications	Design	Coding	Maintenance	Reverse Engineering

Requirements
Matrix Collection
  Matrix
  Manipulation
    Graphical
    Modelling

      Code Management
      Language Aids

        Model Regenerators

Representative CASE tools at lifecycle stages.

The problem is exaggerated further by the iterative nature of the computer software development process. That is, many passes are made at each stage, with input not only from the preceding stage but from subsequent stages. Due to these inefficiencies, most organizations who have attempted to integrate their CASE tools have quickly abandoned the "whole life cycle" idea.

The solution

The AllCASE Integration Framework provides the solution to the integration problem. Through highly efficient metadata-linking algorithms and a highly effective, transaction-based, object-oriented repository, "live links" are built among each tool's data; this provides automatic linkage of data from a given tool with that of other tools. Through adherence to the emerging *Portable Common Tools Environment* (PCTE) integration framework standard, tools from any vendor which conform to the PCTE integration policies can be included quickly and effortlessly in an AllCASE environment.

The marketplace

The following table shows various I-CASE market projects from leading computer industry market survey firms and consultants; the I-CASE marketplace is one of the fastest growing of all computer technologies:

I-CASE Revenue Forecasts (in $ Millions)

	1991	1992	1993	1994	1995
CASE Review	$12	$25	$56	$123	$198
DataCASE	$ 8	$20	$25	$ 45	$126
Mel's CASE	$ 9	$28	$58	$132	$215
REX	$12	$27	$52	$108	$187
Average	$10.25	$25	$47.75	$102	$181.5

Competition

The competition faced by AllCase, Inc. in the I-CASE marketplace can be divided into three main categories: (1) other startup companies, (2) existing CASE vendors extending their offerings to provide integration platforms, and (3) major hardware/system vendors diversifying into the marketplace.

Other startup companies[2]

GroupCASE, Ltd. GroupCASE is a British company, headquartered in London. The company was founded in 1989 by former employees of Monolithic Computers, Inc. (discussed below). GroupCASE is a private company, so little concrete financial information is available regarding the firm's profitability. It is believed that their revenue to date has been about the same as that of AllCase, Inc.

GroupCASE has close marketing ties to Monolithic Computers on the basis of the ties of the company's principals with their former employer. Industry rumor is that GroupCASE's initial integration platform will appear in Q3FY92, and will be marketed by Monolithic Computers, possibly in an exclusive arrangement.

The presentations made by GroupCASE engineers at CASE conferences have tended to be somewhat superficial, so little is known about their specific integration technologies and methodologies.

CASE vendors

DesignMate, Inc. DesignMate, Inc. has been a leader in graphical conceptual database design tools since 1982. In 1987, the Design-Mate product added capabilities to produce *data flow diagrams* (DFDs) and other process-oriented modeling techniques. Initially, the process and data molding techniques did not share any design data due to a lack of integration capabilities. In 1989, DesignMate V4.0 added crude integration capabilities through a limited-function repository with active notification of design data changes. These integration capabilities were only for DesignMate's toolset; no "foreign" tools were integrated.

DesignMate embarked on a wide scale integration program in early 1990, shortly after the release of V4.0. Industry reports have stated that there have been a great deal of retrofitting problems for the existing tools and their current integration methods. Design-Mate reportedly has attempted to provide dual integration methods

(V4.0 plus a new wider scale method that permits foreign tools to be included via published interfaces). V5.0 originally was scheduled for release in July 1991, but has slipped several times. Current estimates are for Q3FY93 at the earliest.

Hardware and system vendors[3]

Monolithic Computers, Inc. Monolithic originally started several CASE tool programs through different areas of the corporation; these programs began in 1984 (data modeling) and 1985 (process modeling). Many of the principals of GroupCASE, Ltd. (discussed earlier) worked on one or both of these efforts.

Monolithic originally announced an ambitious I-CASE program in early 1988, but abandoned that effort in late 1990. It is unlikely that Monolithic will reenter the market, preferring instead to form strategic partnerships with GroupCASE and possibly other I-CASE vendors. Nearly all of the technical and product management leaders involved in their I-CASE program have left the company, and no major announcements of strategic hirings in this area have occurred. It is possible that Monolithic could purchase part or all of an independent I-CASE vendor—either a startup or an existing vendor—but their company acquisitions have slowed since early 1991.

The AllCASE Product

The *AllCASE Integration Framework* (AIR, for short) consists of the following components:

1. *A basic CASE toolset that covers all areas of the development lifecycle.* AIF contains tools developed internally at AllCASE, as well as tools acquired from independent leaders in various life cycle areas. Each tool is capable of processing input from the repository (discussed later), has graphic design and manipulation capabilities, and produces output that is stored in the repository.

2. *An IRDS-compliant repository.* Users can use the AllCASE repository if they choose, or substitute any other IRDS-compliant repository. The repository functions as the *common storage layer* for all AllCASE and integrated tools.

3. *A tool notification manager (TNM).* The TNM is responsible for all integration of design data from participating tools, as well as the "live links" among the tools to notify other participants of changes in design data that must be propagated in other tools.

4. *A tool integration kit (TIK).* The TIK permits CASE tools from any other vendor to be integrated into the AllCASE framework. The TIK assists CASE vendors in providing data sharing and notification mechanisms to their tools compliant with the AIR.

Product advantages

1. The AIF is compliant with all applicable standards efforts: IRDS (repository) and PCTE (tool integration). Through this adherence to standards, integration of other vendors' tools can be accomplished more rapidly than if proprietary interfaces had to be developed.

2. The AIF is being developed on the OSF/1 operating system, which will enhance portability among operating platforms and provide client/server capabilities, remote procedure calls (RPCs), and other technologically advanced features to the product.

3. The AIF permits the concurrent engineering paradigm, with object-oriented characteristics such as long transactions and check-in/check-out, to be undertaken by large, *distributed* design teams.

AllCASE, Inc.: The Company

AllCASE, Inc. was founded in February 1990. The corporate head-quarters are in Tucson, Arizona. Currently, the firm employs 46 professionals. The key personnel and their qualifications are listed below.

Key personnel

Keith Sanders, Chairman and Chief Executive Officer. Keith Sanders founded AllCASE in February, 1990, following 12 years working with various companies in the CASE tools area. Mr. Sanders was director of CASE research at ByteSize, Inc. from 1981 to 1986. Under his direction, ByteSize developed and marketed some of the earliest tools integration technology in the industry. Mr. Sanders then became Vice President of Operations and Chief Operating Officer at Susquehanna Software, Inc., where his responsibilities included CASE products, object-oriented programs, and repository development. Mr. Sanders holds a B.S. in computer science from Stanford University and an M.S. in management information systems from the University of Arizona.

Larry Hogan, Chief Operating Officer. Larry Hogan joined AllCASE one week after the company was incorporated, following a 20-year career at Monolithic Computers, Inc. Mr. Hogan originally was a hardware design engineer, and rose through the ranks at Monolithic to become Vice President of CASE Marketing. Mr. Hogan holds a Ph.D. in computer science from Carnegie-Mellon University and has published over 30 papers on CASE technology, 14 of which have dealt with I-CASE topics.

Suellen Greenfield, Director of Product Development. Suellen Greenfield is one of the foremost educational experts in CASE, having spend 10 years on the faculty of Northern Western University. Ms. Greenfield has authored and presented numerous papers on CASE and related topics, and led a multiuniversity effort to develop the first I-CASE prototype in North America. Her program leadership on that effort resulted in her best-selling book, *Distributed Development of Distributed Software* (Bitfiddle Press, 1987). Ms. Greenfield joined AllCASE in May 1990, in her current position.

Board of directors

Keith Sanders, AllCASE CEO, Chairman of the Board, (602) 555-5858.
Mr. Sanders' biography is presented above.

Francine Giorty, Professor of Computer Science, Treeville University, (810) 555-1111. Dr. Giorty is an acknowledged expert in I-CASE, and has provided valuable steering guidance to the AllCASE development team based on her constant tracking of the latest university-based I-CASE efforts.

Marvin Cash, Managing Partner, Battery Partners, Inc., (710) 555-0000. Mr. Cash is one of the leading venture capital executives in the software industry. Battery Partners is one of the primary investors in AllCASE, and Mr. Cash has provided valuable guidance in many areas, ranging from strategic planning to day-to-day operations and financial planning.

Jarvis Light, Chief Executive Officer, LookAtMe Software, Inc., (200) 555-9999. Mr. Light is the founder and CEO of one of the leading graphical user interface (GUI) PC desktop window and multitasking systems.

Corporate locations

AllCASE, Inc. corporate headquarters is in an office park in Tucson, Arizona. Forty of the 46 employees work at this location. The company also maintains four marketing offices, one each in the following locations:

Location	No. of employees
San Jose, CA	2
New York, NY	1
Dallas, TX	2
Miami, FL	1

Each marketing location is located in an "incubatorlike" building, with a leased office and shared administrative support. The average monthly operating cost of each marketing location is $750, exclusive of salaries and travel costs. Each marketing location is responsible for customer, strategic partner, and other relationships in its geographical area. All offices, and their employees, fall under the supervision of Ms. Olive Vine, the AllCASE director of marketing.

Development environment[4]

All developers of the *AllCASE Integration Framework* (AIF) work in a state-of-the-art development environment, consisting of a system which meets or exceeds the following capabilities:

- OSF/1-based color workstation with 1280X1280 resolution
- 500-Mb local disk storage
- 32-Mb RAM
- 33-MHz clock speed
- Connection to the Development Local Area Network (DevLAN), which features a file server with 3-Gb disk space and 128-Mb RAM.
- Local software for code library management
- Early *full-functioned* prototypes of the *AllCASE Integration Framework* individual tools.[5]

Finances

The following pages contain pertinent financial information, both historical and projected, for AllCASE, Inc. Appendix A contains explanations for all assumptions and the basis for all projections.[6]

AllCASE, Inc.
Balance Sheet
December 31, 1991

Assets		Liabilities and Shareholders' Equity	
Current Assets		Current Liabilities	
Cash and equivalents	$1,750,000	Accounts payable	$ 250,000
Receivables	$ 50,000	Accrued payroll	$ 154,000
Total Current Assets	$1,800,000	Other accrued liabilities	$ 12,000
Property and equipment		Capital Lease Obligations	$ 200,000
Equipment	$ 55,500		
Assets with capital		Long-Term Liabilities	
lease	$ 345,000	Subordinated	
Furniture and fixtures	$ 36,000	debentures, 8%, 10-	
Less: Accumulated		year term	$1,200,000
depreciation	($ 145,000)		
Net Property and		Shareholders' Equity	
Equipment	$291,500	Preferred stock, par	
		value 20¢, 10,000,000	
		shares authorized	
		Series #1, 2,000,000	
		outstanding	$2,000,000
		Accumulated Deficit	($1,724,500)
		Total Liabilities plus	
Total Assets	$2,091,500	Shareholders' Equity	$2,091,500

AllCASE, Inc.
Profit/Loss Statement
Year Ended December 31, 1991

Revenue	$ 124,000
Less Expenses	
Research and development	$ 235,000
General and administrative	$ 623,000
Interest expense	$ 145,000
Total Expenses	$1,003,000
Net Loss	($ 879,000)

AllCASE, Inc.
Projected 3-Year Cash Flow
(Quarterly)

	1992Q1	1992Q2	1992Q3	1992Q4	1993Q1	1993Q2	1993Q3	1993Q4	1994Q1	1994Q2	1994Q3	1994Q4
Beginning Cash	1,750,000	839,000	81,150	4,073,841	3,014,319	4,152,683	2,943,935	1,708,555	401,110	675,169	2,980,408	6,116,256
Inflows												
Cash sales plus Accounts receivable Collections	34,000	36,000	38,000	40,000	45,000	50,000	135,000	185,000	1,900,000	4,200,000	5,350,000	6,500,000
Investment capital			5,000,000		2,250,000							
Short-term debt		200,000										
Less												
Salaries	−690,000	−724,500	−760,725	−798,761	−838,699	−922,569	−1,014,826	−1,116,309	−1,227,940	−1,473,528	−1,768,233	−2,121,880
Capital lease payments	−125,000	−132,500	−140,450	−148,877	−157,810	−167,278	−177,315	−187,954	−199,231	−211,185	−223,856	−237,287
General and administrative expenses	−85,000	−90,950	−97,317	−104,129	−111,418	−119,217	−127,562	−136,491	−146,046	−156,269	−167,208	−178,912
Other payments and expenses	−45,000	−45,900	−46,818	−47,754	−48,709	−49,684	−50,677	−51,691	−52,725	−53,779	−54,855	−55,952
Ending Cash	839,000	81,150	4,073,841	3,014,319	4,152,683	2,943,935	1,708,555	401,110	675,169	2,980,408	6,116,256	10,022,225

AllCASE, Inc.
3-Year Profit/Loss Projection
1992–1994

	1992	1993	1994
Revenue	$ 145,000	$ 224,000	$21,400,000
Less Expenses			
Research and development	$ 545,000	$ 675,000	$ 725,000
General and administrative	$ 822,000	$ 979,000	$17,730,000
Interest expense	$ 145,000	$ 145,000	$ 145,000
Selling expenses	$ 65,000	$ 175,000	$ 450,000
Total Expenses	$1,577,000	$1,974,000	$19,050,000
Net Profit/(Loss)	($1,432,000)	($1,750,000)	$ 2,350,000

AllCASE, Inc.
Current Year Quarterly Head Count Plan
1992

	1992 Q1	1992 Q2	1992 Q3	1992 Q4
Beginning Head Count	46	52	55	61
Development	5	2	4	6
Sales and Marketing	0	1	1	4
General and Administrative	1	0	1	1
Ending Head Count	52	55	61	72

AllCASE, Inc.
3-Year Head Count Plan
1992–1994

	1992	1993	1994
Beginning Head Count	46	72	101
Development	17	12	14
Sales and Marketing	6	9	16
General and Administrative	3	8	9
Ending Head Count	72	101	140

Investment

AllCASE, Inc. is seeking $7,500,000 in investment capital. The timing of the portions of this investment is listed below.

Amount	Period
$5,000,000	Q3 1992
$2,250,000	Q1 1993

Additional References

1. Mr. Bill Whearton
   CASE Consulting Group (CCG)
   1 Wilson Plaza
   New York, NY 10000
   (212) 555-3333

2. Ms. Nancy Wall
   Venture Partners
   333 Diamond Blvd.
   Honolulu, Hawaii 90000
   (515) 555-2222

3. Mr. Michael Filmer
   Professor of Computer Science
     and Department Chairman
   Northern Western University
   444 Main Street
   Yuma, AZ 89000
   (602) 555-7777

Business Plan End Notes

1. We have not included page numbers in the Table of Contents since this sample business plan falls into the middle of the book; a real-life business plan would list the page numbers for each section.
2. In the interest of space, we have included only one sample company from each category. In a real-life business plan, there would probably be three to four entries per category. *The key is to be as complete as possible, especially in business plans seeking financing.*
3. A thorough business plan competitive analysis should also discuss companies who no longer are considered competitors (such as in this case), as well as possible newcomers. While a business plan should not extensively revolve around rumors, discussion of trade reports and other public information regarding strategic partnerships, possible buyouts, and related matters is valuable to the readers.
4. In some cases, particularly those dealing with software development, it may be desirable to include a description of the development environment so that prospective investors can see that all applicable efforts are being made to provide a highly productive investment.
5. Whenever possible, try to show that the product in which you would like someone to invest is being used in its early stages; this lends credibility to the product itself, and therefore to the business plan.
6. It is desirable to include as detailed an explanation as possible regarding the basis of projections, growth rates, and other pertinent information. We have not included a sample appendix as referenced in this sample business plan.

9

Writing
Product Development
Support Documents

Introduction

The software development-related documents discussed in the preceding chapters—those dealing with requirements, specifications, documentation, and so on—are applicable to development efforts in many different types of organizations, both vendor and user. While vendor-developed software usually is intended for use in other companies, and user-developed software typically is used internally, the same development life cycle applies to both of those efforts.

There are, however, added responsibilities and functions in vendor organizations that usually don't apply to user-developed software programs. These have to do with the production and introduction of commercial software, and each function has a corresponding document type that must be written by a computer professional within that company. These responsibilities, and their corresponding documents, include:

- Marketing: marketing plan
- Initial product introduction: product introduction plan
- Internal and external testing: testing plan
- Copyright, trademark, patent, and trade secret protection: legal protection strategy plan
- Training for internal support personnel and customers: training plan

- International activities: international activities plan
- Development of user documentation: documentation plan
- Customer support: customer support plan

In this chapter, we'll take a detailed look at several of the above product support plans, including sample document portions. Though many vendor organizations are trying to streamline their software development process in light of corporate downsizings, the functions mentioned above nonetheless are critical and the accompanying documentation important to the overall activities. Because of the aforementioned downsizings and other consolidation efforts, many computer professionals find themselves charged with writing one or more of the plans discussed in this chapter, whereas in the past the responsibilities would have been assigned to "specialists." Therefore, it is helpful to at least be familiar with the types of documents discussed in this chapter in case you are ever assigned such a task.

Those readers with experience at vendors may be familiar with the phase-oriented product development process, in which each development phase is accompanied by a massive compilation of documents, including those shown later in this chapter. *It is strongly recommended that in order to maximize the number of people who will actually read a product development support document you may write, verbiage should be minimized to keep document sizes as small as possible.* Reviewers are more likely to study compact documents than wordy, lengthy ones, when they are faced with reviewing 15 or 20 documents over a three-week span. Try to include all relevant information, but as concisely as possible.

Each document should have a *brief* product description at or near the beginning. While a lengthy description may be found in the business plan or a related product description document, never assume that readers of any given plan will have access to or bother to read the document in which that material is located.

Additionally, while the business plan and/or product development plan contain detailed, comprehensive schedules for all activities, each plan should feature an abbreviated schedule with such relevant information as product introduction date and all activities pertinent to the activity covered by that plan (marketing, legal protection, and so forth).

Cautions

When tasked with developing any of the product development support plans discussed in this chapter, it is often tempting to take one or more existing plans from other products within the company and make minor modifications, primarily in schedules and other obvious areas, to produce the required document. To reiterate our warning from the first chapter, *we strongly caution that this approach is usually not desirable; such practices often lead to inadequate and unsuccessful products being developed.* The rapid changes so obvious in the computer industry with respect to technology are also evident in other areas, including those covered by support plans discussed in this chapter. While the urge to reduce the amount of work by borrowing from existing plans may be tempting, situations and environments often change rapidly, and these changes should be reflected in the current document. For example:

- How does a recent court ruling on software copyright protection affect the current product's legal protection strategy? This court ruling may not have been in effect when previous legal protection strategy documents were developed, and failure to account for this may be detrimental.

- How do on-line information retrieval mechanisms affect the documentation plan? Recent advances in hypertext may cause more documentation resources to be oriented towards on-line documentation than traditional bound volumes.

- What new trade shows and periodicals have risen to prominence? Those referenced in older marketing and product introduction plans may no longer exist or may have been merged with other similar sources.

Again, the point is that each situation should be examined carefully in its own light and corollary documents should reflect "reality" as it currently exists. Too much reliance on boilerplate documents serves little purpose other than to accelerate the document production process; the resulting substance almost always is corrupted by this method.

Marketing Plan

The marketing plan, as should be obvious from its title, is a detailed discussion of all marketing-related activities dealing with (in our context) a computer-related product. In many circumstances, the marketing plan is folded into the business plan (Chap. 8). It is recommended, however, and indeed it is common practice among many vendors, that you develop a separate marketing plan with appropriate references in the business plan.

The four major principles of marketing—product, price, promotion, and place/distribution—should all be discussed in the marketing plan with respect to the product at hand. For those readers with little formal business training, we must add a brief statement here: Marketing is not identical to advertising. While advertising strategies (discussed later) should indeed be discussed in the marketing plan, the discipline of marketing encompasses far more than advertising. Each of the above principles is crucial in its own way to the success of a product, and each can be tied directly into marketing activities.

A typical marketing plan should include the following sections:

1. *A description of the product.* This should be from the "marketing angle" rather than from a technical vantage point. That is, an applications software package should be described in terms of its major functions, the vertical or horizontal market it serves, and other related aspects, rather than the program structure, development language, or other technical issues that are of little concern to the marketing activities.

2. *Issues related to pricing.* While the business plan will deal with forecasts and related projections, the marketing plan should designate the overall pricing strategy: price penetration (for example, a relatively low price intended to quickly secure market share); or price skimming (for example, a relatively high price intended to reflect a premium product positioning strategy). If appropriate, marketing-oriented discount structures and other pricing items should be included.

3. *The distribution strategy.* Software products may be sold through many different channels, such as a direct sales force, mail-order, distributors and/or retailers, or in other ways. Depending on which channel(s) are being utilized, the distribution strategy, and related marketing activities, will differ. These should be discussed in detail.

4. *The promotion strategies.* Typically, this section comprises one of the, if not the single, largest portions of the marketing plan. In this section all activities related to advertising *and other promotional means* are discussed, with detailed costs and budgets, appropriate media outlets, major marketing messages, and other items. Given the numerous promotional activities, and the widely varying cost structures of each, a coordinated, carefully orchestrated promotional strategy is essential to maximize the transmission of marketing messages to potential customers.

5. *Coordination plan.* Many vendors, particularly hardware-oriented firms, have several types of marketing groups, such as industry-specific marketing, product group marketing, government marketing, and so on. As is typical in many large organizations, there is a tremendous amount of overlap among these organizations, as well as certain activities which always seem to fall through the cracks by not "officially" belonging to any one organization. The marketing plan

should outline the responsibilities of each and every marketing organization within the company, and should strive to provide verification mechanisms to ensure that all activities are carried out as necessary by the group assigned the task.

6. *Strategic relationship marketing (if applicable)*. Many of today's product development efforts, both hardware and software, involve two or more companies working together. The marketing organizations from each participating company should be involved in the marketing activities, and therefore the product marketing plan should ensure that all intercompany activities are coordinated and do not conflict with one another. It is extremely important to ensure that all companies understand, agree with, and utilize the same marketing messages, promotional activities, and other marketing tasks.

Sample marketing plan

A portion of a sample marketing plan is presented below.

MightyWord Corp.
Product Introduction Plan
MightyWord V1.0
February 15, 1992

Revision History:

2/15/92, First Draft: Bob Treadwell

Address comments to: Bob Treadwell, Product Marketing, 555-5555

Comments due by: 3/1/92

1   Product Description and Related Schedule

MightyWord is a complete document and text management system that operates under a client/server architecture. Users, interfacing with the *graphical user interface* (GUI) client software, can perform functions such as word processing, spell checking, and hypertext keyword processing with many different server-based relational database management systems. MightyWord is unique in the software marketplace because of the integrated nature of its components and its ability to utilize an active notification repository.

MightyWord V1.0 is scheduled for initial customer shipments on October 12, 1992. The following announcement schedule, adapted from the MightyWord Business Plan, applies to all marketing activities:

April 21, 1992: Approval of marketing plan

July 2, 1992: Preannouncement activities begin

August 22, 1992: Official product announcement

October 12, 1992: Initial customer shipment

Further product information, including a detailed list of features, is included in the MightyWord Business Plan.

2 Pricing

Although MightyWord is a unique software package, the nature of its host computing environment—personal computers and other low-end desktop systems—requires a pricing strategy in line with most personal computer word processing software. Because of the added value of MightyWord as compared to an "ordinary" word processing program, the high end of the pricing spectrum—$750–$900 list price—is a viable target.

3 Distribution

MightyWord will be sold through several different channels. The primary distribution channel is through computer retailers, primarily the national and regional chains. MightyWord may be sold in quantity to the large chains themselves, or to software distributors who typically service smaller chains and individual stores.

Additionally, MightyWord can be sold through the direct sales forces of large hardware vendors who have an active cooperative marketing plan. At initial release an agreement will be in place between MightyWord Corp. and MMCS (Massively Monolothic Computer Systems) whereby the MMCS sales force will have catalog access to MightyWord software. For this reason, cooperative marketing (discussed later in this plan) between MMCS and MightyWord Corp. will provide for coordinated trade show appearances, cooperative advertising, and other joint marketing efforts.

4 Promotion Strategy

The business plan authorizes the market department to spend $750,000 for first-year marketing activities, including all paid advertising. Many of the activities listed below constitute no-charge or low-cost promotional means (press releases, interviews, and so forth) and should be maximized. The initial promotional activities are discussed in more detail in the MightyWord V1.0 Product Introduction Plan.*

---

*A sample product introduction plan is included in the next section.

The promotional activities for MightyWord V1.0 include the following:

Activity	Point of contact	Sources	Start date
Press releases; "pre-announcement"	Product Marketing (Bob Treadwell)	Trade periodicals Business magazines Major metropolitan newspapers	July 31, 1992
Advertising	XYZ Advertising Agency; Corporate Advertising (Mike Marion)	Trade periodicals Business magazines In-store ad displays	May 1, 1992: planning Aug. 22, 1992: first ads appear
Official press release	Product Marketing (Bob Treadwell)	Trade periodicals Business magazines Major metropolitan newspapers	Aug. 22, 1992
Trade shows	Product Marketing (Bob Treadwell)	PC Software Expo Word Processors of America International Software Expo	Aug. 31, 1992
Direct mail marketing	Product Marketing (Bob Treadwell)	Periodical-sponsored card decks Flyers/marketing letters	Aug. 22, 1992

5 Marketing Activities Coordination

Three organizations within MightyWord Corp. have responsibility for marketing activities for MightyWord V1.0. They are

Marketing organization	Point of contact
Product Marketing	Bob Treadwell, 555-5555
Industry Marketing	Steve Stevens, 555-7777
Corporate Advertising	Mike Marion, 555-7778

The Product Marketing organization will be the focal point for all marketing activities for MightyWord V1.0; all activities will be coordinated by Bob Treadwell or a designated alternative point of contact. All contacts with external advertising agencies will be coordinated by the Corporate Advertising organization. All advertisements will be approved by Product Marketing to ensure that the major marketing messages are correctly presented.

Product Introduction Plan

Ideally, the product introduction plan should be preceded by the marketing plan, since nearly all of the product introduction activities are directly related to and determined by the marketing strategy. Often, the two plans are developed in parallel due to schedule considerations and other factors. In these circumstances, the development of the two plans should be an iterative process, with each document drawing from the ideas of the other. While several cycles usually are warranted for any of the documents discussed in this chapter and in the book, there will likely be an increased number of iterations of the marketing and product introduction plans because of the dependencies of one upon the other.

The product introduction plan should include all of the activities directly related to the initial introduction of the product, while the marketing plan discusses the overall marketing strategy throughout the product life cycle. Each of the items discussed in the product introduction plan should be described in *extensive* detail, as compared with the somewhat general nature of the marketing plan.

Items in the product introduction plan may include:

- Trade shows and conferences at which the product will be featured, and in what form (presentations, product booths, and so on)

- Specific magazines, newspapers, journals, and other media outlets in which advertising, press releases, and other publicity will be generated and featured

- Specific direct marketing, direct mail, and other related activities; the target audiences, expected responses, sources (generated within the company or by an outside agency or other form)

- Customer-specific presentations

- Contingency plans at various points within the product introduction strategy if expected results are not achieved

Additionally, the product introduction plan should discuss the specific individuals involved in the various activities, particularly those events such as seminars and customer presentations which require time from those involved in other activities. It should never be assumed automatically, for example, that the lead software developers will spend three or four days at a conference or seminar, or be "on call" for customer presentations in remote cities, unless that scheduling is coordinated with other activities such as external test support. *In this way, the product introduction plan helps to facilitate the overall resource management process by forcing recognition of expected time and other commitments across activities.*

Sample product introduction plan

A portion of a sample product introduction plan is presented below.

MightyWord Corp.
Product Marketing Plan
MightyWord V1.0
February 15, 1992

Revision History:

2/15/92, First Draft: Bob Treadwell

Address comments to: Bob Treadwell, Product Marketing, 555-5555

Comments due by: 3/1/92

1 Product Description and Related Schedule

MightyWord is a complete document and text management system that operates under a client/server architecture. Users, interfacing with the *graphical user interface* (GUI) client software, can perform functions such as word processing, spell checking, and hypertext keyword processing with many different server-based relational database management systems. MightyWord is unique in the software marketplace because of the integrated nature of its components and its ability to utilize an active notification repository.

MightyWord V1.0 is scheduled for initial customer shipments on October 12, 1992. The following announcement schedule, adapted from the MightyWord Business Plan, applies to all product introduction activities:

April 21, 1992: Approval of marketing and product introduction plans

July 2, 1992: Preannouncement activities begin; begin customer briefings

August 22, 1992: Official product announcement; begin trade shows and other "official" activities related to product introduction

October 12, 1992: Initial customer shipment

April 1, 1993: End official product introduction period

Further product information, including a detailed list of features, is included in the MightyWord Business Plan.

2 Customer Briefings and Presentations

Customer briefings constitute an important part of the product introduction activities. Twenty potential customers have been identified by the MightyWord Corp. marketing and product management organizations as being candidates as strategic partners. A number of nondisclosure briefings have been under way since early 1991, primarily from the technology exchange viewpoint. Beginning in February 1992, the nondisclosure briefings will shift to a product-specific orientation respective to MightyWord V1.0.

Each customer briefing will follow the guidelines listed below:

1. All briefings will be coordinated by Bob Treadwell or a designated alternative in the Marketing department. No requests from customers will come directly to developers, even in follow-up situations, since the overwhelming goal of engineering is meeting the development schedule. Subject to their schedules, developers will be assigned to respective customers along with a person from Marketing or Product Management.

2. Each briefing will follow the appropriate nondisclosure agreement guidelines as outlined by MightyWord Legal.

3. Each briefing will be oriented toward the goal of facilitating a strategic relationship with the customer; this will include product endorsements and other activities.

3 Trade Shows

One of the primary introduction strategies for MightyWord V1.0 is to attend *all* applicable trade shows. The schedule for 1992-1993 (through 2/93) is listed below. Additional trade shows will be added at appropriate points throughout this period.

Trade show	Dates	Attendee(s)	MightyWord activity
PC Software Expo	Aug. 31–Sept. 2, 1992	Treadwell Melbourne	Booth
Word Processors of America	Sept. 29–30, 1992	Melbourne Walters	Presentation; booth
International Software Expo	Oct. 12–15, 1992	Melbourne (?)developer	Booth; courtesy suite
Winter PC Software Expo	Dec. 15–18, 1992	Treadwell	Booth; panel lead
ABC Word Utilities	Jan. 12, 1993	Melbourne	Presentation; booth
Large Word Show	Feb. 15, 1993	Treadwell Young (?)developer	Booth; courtesy suite

4 Conferences and Seminars

There are four conferences scheduled for 1992–1993 in which presentations of papers by MightyWord Corp. engineers would be of immense value to the product introduction process. The first two are already scheduled, and the papers have been submitted for approval.

Conference	Dates	Attendee(s)	Subject	Status
Textual Algorithms 1992	Mar. 28–30, 1992	Michaels	Search algorithms	Submitted; awaiting approval
HyperInformation 1992	Apr. 15–18, 1992	Williams	HyperInformation integration	Submitted; awaiting approval
Client/Server Word Processing	Sept. 18–20, 1992	Michaels	Client/server WP	Being written
Enterprise Word Processing 1993	Jan. 18–20, 1993	Williams	Heterogeneous WIP	Being written

5 Advertising

Initial advertising efforts will concentrate on trade periodicals oriented towards personal computers, as well as a selected number of general computing magazines and newspapers. General business periodical advertising will follow approximately six months after product announcement; these plans are currently under development and will be completed by April 15, 1992. The tentative advertising schedule and budget is listed below.

Publication	Issue	Size	Budget
Word Processing Magazine	9/15/92, then weekly afterwards for 12 weeks	Full page	$6,000 ea.
Word Processing Magazine	9/22/92	6 page adv. supplement	$12,000
Software and Systems	9/23/92	Full page	$5,500
PC Software World	9/24/92	Half-page	$3,200
Microsoftware Review	9/30/92, then biweekly afterwards for 8 issues	Full page	$5,800 ea.
MightyWord Magazine	Initial issue 9/22/92; monthly	Six pages ea. issue	$12,000 ea. issue*
This Week in Business	3/15/93	Advertising supplement (est. 8 pp.)	$18,700

*Internal funds transfer.

6 Press Releases

The official MightyWord V1.0 press release will be sent to more than 275 publications. The complete list is shown in Attachment A.* All press releases will be submitted by the MightyWord Corp. advertising organization, following coordination and approval by marketing, product management, and development. There will be three forms of press releases:

1. A ½-page version, with only a brief description of the product, the major marketing messages, and release date information

2. A 2-page version, which will include the above information plus a list of major features

3. A 6-page version, based on the paid advertising supplements being prepared, which will include product information, features, and the following:

   - "Technology" articles that correspond to the major features of MightyWord V1.0
   - Testimonials and endorsements from external test site users
   - Annotated color photographs of GUI screens
   - A comparative specification sheet showing MightyWord V1.0 versus competition

Product Testing Plan

In the context of product development support documents, the product testing plan is not the same as the type with which most programmers are familiar. The latter form usually consists of procedures, expected results, exception handling, and other information pertaining to module testing, unit testing, system-wide testing, and other development-related activities; this type of testing plan is intended to provide guidance to those attempting to ascertain product "correctness."

In our current context, the testing plan is intended to detail the methodology for testing the entire product, both within the company and at selected customers sites. By "methodology" we mean all prerequisite and corequisite activities that deal with the external testing (often called "beta testing") and internal testing procedures. Rather than provide the testers with a formal list of software (or hardware)

---

*This is just an example; Attachment A to the sample product introduction plan is not included here. Note, however, that extremely lengthy lists, such as the one referenced here, which may fill several pages often are best suited for inclusion in plans as attachments to avoid disruption of the flow of the document.

testing steps, as in the case of the other type of testing plan, our plan will give general guidelines for different testing organizations and will list support mechanisms and other required activities. These items include:

- The type of organizations and customers, in terms of their levels of experience with similar products (or earlier versions of the same product, if the current product being developed is an enhanced version of an existing product)

- Prerequisite hardware, software, operating environments, and other factors required to successfully conduct testing

- If applicable and if early testing feedback is desired, testing of parts of the product

- Required training for users and test support personnel

- Geographical dispersion of testing organizations, particularly if the product has international facets (multiple languages, and so on)

- Problem reporting mechanisms (on-line error reporting; phone support; and so on)

- "Correctness" reporting mechanisms (What was tested? What worked without error?)

- The distribution means to the testing organizations for original and modified products

- How many internal and external testing organizations should be utilized

- Applicable schedules

Sample product testing plan

Portions of a sample product testing plan are presented below.

MightyWord Corp.
Product Testing Plan
MightyWord V1.0
February 15, 1992

Revision History:

2/15/92, First Draft: Ann Williams

Address comments to: Ann Williams, Product Testing Administration, 555-9876

Comments due by: 3/1/92

1 Product Description and Related Schedule

MightyWord is a complete document and text management system that operates under a client/server architecture. Users, interfacing with the *graphical user interface* (GUI) client software, can perform functions such as word processing, spell checking, and hypertext keyword processing with many different server-based relational database management systems. MightyWord is unique in the software marketplace because of the integrated nature of its components and its ability to utilize an active notification repository.

MightyWord V1.0 is scheduled for initial customer shipments on October 12, 1992. The following announcement schedule, adapted from the MightyWord Business Plan, applies to all testing activities:

February 1, 1992: Selection of internal testing sites (already completed)

March 5, 1992: Final selection of external testing sites (already in progress at this writing)

March 10, 1992: Internal test site training

March 15, 1992: Distribution of software to internal testing sites

April 1, 1992: External test site training

April 15, 1992: Distribution of software to external testing sites

June 1, 1992: Expected distribution of modified software to testing sites

August 1, 1992: End of testing period

Further product information, including a detailed list of features, is included in the MightyWord Business Plan.

2 Site Testing Qualifications and Criteria

Five internal organizations within MightyWord Corp. have been selected as internal test sites, with a total of 25 users (5 per organization). Four companies will be selected as external test sites from a finalist list of twelve corporations. It is expected that a total of 25 to 30 external users will participate in test use.

Within each category, internal and external, experience levels will vary among the users. Approximate numbers within each experience level category are shown below. It is critical that users from various levels of the experience spectrum be selected since MightyWord will be used by people with correspondingly broad experience levels.

Experience level	Internal	External
No word processing experience	3	3
Moderate word processing experience; basic text editing only	10	11
Advanced word processing experience; spell checking, thesaurus functions, etc.	12	16

Each test site must appoint a single person as the local test coordinator. The test coordinator will be responsible for assisting other users, particularly the novice users, and coordinating the problem-reporting procedures with the MightyWord technical staff.

No international features will be present in MightyWord V1.0. Therefore, no international testing is required. To simplify training, testing administration, and problem resolution during the relatively short time period allotted, the testing locations for companies (rather than their corporate headquarters) selected as external test sites should be located no more than 150 miles from the MightyWord development facility in Philadelphia.

3 Prerequisite Testing Environments

All individual users must have the following minimum testing configuration:

- IBM-compatible personal computer, 80286 or greater processor, 16 MhZ clock speed recommended
- MS-DOS 3.0 or greater
- 40 Mb hard disk
- 640 Kb memory
- Connection to Ethernet local area network
- TCP/IP software

Additionally, each test site must have a file server with an identical configuration to that listed above, except the file server must have a minimum of 150 Mb hard disk space, plus a modem and communications software (the latter two items for problem reporting).

4 Training

The MightyWord training department is evaluating multiple training methods. The testing process for MightyWord V1.0 will contain three types of testing:

Testing type	No. of internal people	No. of external people
One-day classroom training session	8	10
"Introduction to MightyWord" manual only	8	10
Computer-assisted training material	9	10

The one-day classroom session will be prepared and conducted by the MightyWord training staff in conjunction with the customer training course under development.

5   Reporting Procedures

All users involved in the testing process will be given on-line problem reporting forms. The forms may be completed using any word processing or text editing package with which users are familiar, although they will be encouraged to use MightyWord V1.0 (unless the problem found is too severe to use the test software). Each form is accompanied by trigger software, which automatically will send a copy to the file server. The test administrator for each site should submit any problem reports collected on the server to MightyWord Corp. within 48 hours, and will subsequently be responsible for problem duplication. Test administrators will also be responsible for notifying the reporting user of the problem resolution.

Legal Protection Strategy Plan

All commercial software and hardware must have a legal protection strategy as part of its development and introduction process. Items that are included under legal protection include:

- Trademarking of product names, and ensuring that trademarks do not infringe upon those of others
- Registering the copyright of source code
- Applying for and defending any applicable patents
- Protecting all applicable trade secrets, particularly when joint ventures with other companies are undertaken

In most cases, the product manager is responsible for developing the legal protection strategy and the associated document. In turn, many of the activities are assigned to the organization's in-house legal staff. As a caution to the readers, many corporate legal staffs are overburdened with a large number of tasks, particularly because corporations accelerated their downsizing activities of the late 1980s and early 1990s, when many corporate legal staffs were trimmed severely. This trend is likely to continue, or flatten at best, which means that a small cadre of attorneys will be responsible for implementing the items in the legal protection strategy. *It is imperative, therefore, that all assignments outlined in the Legal Protection Strategy be assigned to individual persons whenever possible to help ensure that the tasks are done in a timely manner.* At the very least, specific legal organizations—for example, "Binghamton, N.Y. Trademark Legal Office" rather than "corporate legal"— should be designated as the office of primary responsibility.

Sample legal protection strategy plan

A portion of a sample legal protection strategy plan is presented below.

MightyWord Corp.
Legal Protection Strategy Plan
MightyWord V1.0
February 15, 1992

Revision History:

2/15/92, First Draft: Marv Sandler

Address comments to: Marv Sandler, Product Manager, 555-1111

Comments due by: 3/1/92

1 Product Description and Related Schedule

MightyWord is a complete document and text management system that operates under a client/server architecture. Users, interfacing with the *graphical user interface* (GUI) client software, can perform functions such as word processing, spell checking, and hypertext keyword processing with many different server-based relational database management systems. MightyWord is unique in the software marketplace because of the integrated nature of its components and its ability to utilize an active notification repository.

MightyWord V1.0 is scheduled for initial customer shipments on October 12, 1992. The following announcement schedule, adapted from the MightyWord Business Plan, applies to all legal activities:

January 10, 1992: Conduct trademark search (already completed)

January 15, 1992: Apply for trademark (already completed)

January 15, 1992: Trade secret protection: seminar for all personnel (already completed)

February 28, 1992: Complete all boilerplate nondisclosure forms

February 28, 1992: Submit all engineering patents

August 31, 1992: Submit all required code segments to the U.S. Copyright Office

Further product information, including a detailed list of features, is included in the MightyWord Business Plan.

2 Trade Secrets

All information confidential to MightyWord Corp. must be treated as a trade secret. This includes such items as the existence of MightyWord V1.0 software prior to product preannouncement activities, code algorithms, and plans for future versions. A seminar in trade secret protection has already been presented to the development staff. All documents to date have been marked COMPANY CONFIDENTIAL, and all documents generated will be marked likewise.

All confidential presentations to perspective customers have been under nondisclosure agreement. Presentations until product announcement, as well as any subsequent presentations and discussions that contain material confidential to MightyWord Corp. (such as features in upcoming versions, future operating system platforms, strategic product alliances with other companies), will be done likewise.

All source codes will contain appropriate copyright notices within the body of the code. All documentation will contain appropriate copyright and trademark notices.

Each company selected to serve as an external testing site will be required to sign a nondisclosure agreement. Most of the candidate companies have already received confidential presentations under nondisclosure agreements, and those agreements may be extended to cover the testing process.

The product manager (Marv Sandler) is responsible for coordinating all trade secret protection activities.

3 Patents

Initial review of the algorithms and other technologies has yielded two candidates for patent protection. These have been forwarded to Mike Stein, MightyWord Corp. patent attorney, for further review and application. Until approval of patents or withdrawal of the applications, no references to the patent candidates will be made to anyone outside of MightyWord Corp., even under nondisclosure agreement.

4 Trademark

The trademark search for the product name of "MightyWord" has already been completed. Since MightyWord Corp. owns the trademark of "MightyWord," no problems were anticipated. Following receipt of the official trademark, all references to the product name will use the appropriate™ notation.

Summary

The sample plans presented in this chapter are exceedingly brief in the interest of including as many examples as possible in the allotted space. In reality, most plans would be somewhat longer, but, as was mentioned in this chapter's introduction, only that which is absolutely required should be included. Again, many of these plans go through the same document review cycle at the same time, often with frenzied activity on the part of those most involved in all levels of product development. To ensure that plans are read as thoroughly as possible, they should contain primarily information which requires coordination and approval as well as other pertinent material.

10

Writing to Be Published

At first glance, writing articles, technical papers, and books might appear to be outside the realm of most computer professionals' primary job functions and, thus, outside the scope of career-oriented writing. In reality, many successful computer professionals complement their job functions, and enhance their own career paths, with professional writing. In these tough job times, frequent and successful publications can help distinguish *your* career and possibly provide one of the primary differentiators between continued career success and stagnation.

In this chapter we'll explore the world of commercial writing in the computer field and examine such topics as how to select appropriate channels of publication, orient your writing style and subject matter to best enhance your career, and suggest a number of related guidelines to maximize your effective written communications in the public area.

What Should I Write?

There are several primary channels through which you can pursue professional writing. Within each of those channels are further breakdowns with respect to subject matter, audiences, type of writing, and other categories. These are discussed in greater detail later in the chapter.

Magazine articles

The "simplest," but by no means easiest, places to publish your writing are computer-related magazines such as *Byte, Datamation, PC World,* or similar publications. Alternatively, some subject matter may be applicable to general business or other publications such as inflight airline magazines.

By "simple" we mean that magazine articles have far less restrictive guidelines and rules than technical papers (discussed next), are far more compact, and take less time to write than books. There is a large variety of subjects from which you can write magazine articles about computer-related subjects, (see Fig. 10.1), including:

1. *Writing about new products.* Most computer periodicals publish articles about new hardware, software, peripheral, and support products. As new computers, printers, DBMS software, spreadsheet programs, LANs, and other products appear on the market, a corresponding need arises for articles about these products.

These articles can take various forms, including:

- A thorough review and evaluation of a given product, including a feature-by-feature rating of the product's capabilities.

- Comparative surveys of multiple new products, including those comparing features. For example, you might write an article about three or four new integrated software packages, highlighting and evaluating each program's features and comparing them.

2. *Writing about existing products.* Even products that have been on the market for a while can be discussed in your articles. An article about advanced features of a given product, programming techniques, or other "tips" is likely to be of interest to periodical readers.

3. *Technologies and trends.* Many computer periodicals also publish articles about "new" (to the general computing public) technologies, the uses for those technologies on current and future products, and related trends. If your forte is object-oriented databases, CASE, networks, open systems, or a similar topic, you might query a publisher about writing an article on one of these or other subjects.

Unlike technical papers (discussed in the next subsection), articles about technologies and trends written for general computer publications tend to be tutorial in nature. That is, an article about the latest

1. New Products

2. Existing Products

3. Technologies and Trends

4. Regular Columns

Figure 10.1 Representative categories of magazine articles.

trends in distributed databases should be explanatory rather than of an academic, "proof-intensive" nature. Later in this chapter we'll talk more about the respective types of writing most applicable to various careers. For those who feel more comfortable targeting general publications rather than technical journals, the writing style and subject matter should fit the medium and the audience.

4. *Regular columns.* Many successful writers have gone from writing occasional articles to being featured in regular (weekly, biweekly, monthly) columns in publications. If you have a particular area of expertise, such as UNIX, open systems, or database products, you might try to follow a string of successful articles with a request for a regular column on your area of specialization. If you can find a good match between a publication's needs and your knowledge and experience, you may be able to arrange for a regular column.

Technical papers

Many computer professionals, particularly those working in research environments with leading edge technologies or in academic climates, elect to write technical papers for journals, conference proceedings, or other scholarly outlets. Unlike magazine articles, which tend to be "free-format" (that is, the content, style, and design are dictated primarily by commercial concerns), technical papers—even those of nearly identical subject matter to cousin magazine articles—are far more restrictive in their presentation.

For example, the sample tutorial article about distributed database trends discussed in the previous section would take on a far different appearance if targeted towards a technical journal rather than a general computing magazine. First, you would automatically assume that the reading audience consists almost exclusively of computer professionals (or at least students in a computer-oriented curriculum) rather than a mix of end users and computer generalists (such as PC software developers with little or no distributed database exposure). Correspondingly, a magazine tutorial would likely regress further into discussions of applicable database and distribution fundamentals *within the body of the article itself,* a technical paper, which usually has an introductory paragraph or two with citations to previously published papers, books, and other sources leaves it up to the reader as to whether he or she feels the background information is worth researching.

Secondly, technical papers usually are governed by various restrictions with respect to the content, the proof of concepts, and other characteristics. The author of a magazine article on integrated CASE environments might be able to "free-format daydream" about the optimal, ultimate instantiation of such a platform, while a technical paper usually would have to cite various research projects at universities and companies in this area as sources of the technical information. The journals themselves often have various policies that govern the format, content, and required background research for papers printed in their publications.

For the sake of uniqueness, a magazine article might be written with a humorous flare or in some other manner that makes it stand out from articles in other periodicals. It is unlikely, however, that such a slant could be used technical papers.

Books

Many computer-related subjects—those applicable to general publications as well as technical journal subjects—can be expanded to book-length. Writing a book might appear to be an intimidating prospect; though it is time-consuming, it is well within the capabilities of most well-disciplined computer professionals. In fact, the process of book writing is very similar to developing computer code for medium- to large-scale systems.

Computer books can be similar to magazine articles in that they might be tutorial in nature, product-oriented, or might discuss trends or other subjects of interest to computer professionals. Alternatively, they might be book-length variations of technical papers, flush with formulas, proofs, and other characteristics of academic writing.

We'll talk later about choosing subject matter for computer books; in the meantime, keep in mind that there are many publishers in the computer book field, and with the ongoing rapid changes in computer technology there is a constant need for books about new products, technologies, and other subjects.

How does the subject matter relate to my career?

Getting any article or book published can be of tremendous benefit to your career in the computer field. That benefit, however, can be maximized by careful planning that matches the subject matter to your current or future career goals. If, for example, your current area of expertise is computerized investment analysis, an article, paper, or book with a financial orientation provides a highly useful coupling with your "full-time" career; more so than, for example, a textbook about compiler theory. This is not to denigrate the latter possibility, however; your career goals might include teaching part-time or, eventually, full-time, at a leading university, and the textbook can be a tremendous boost to achieving your goal. Regardless of how close a match there is between your career path and the subject matter about which you write, remember that you still get paid for writing!

Publications Media

Let's take a closer look at the different outlets for your writing that we mentioned in the previous section. Computer magazines and periodicals can be divided into several categories, each with its own distinctive publishing potential for your writing (see Fig. 10.2), including the following:

1. *General.* This category includes such staples as *Computerworld, Datamation,* and *Systems Integration.* You might target to these types of publications an advanced-level article that discusses, for example, how industrial companies are easing their way into using object-oriented technologies.

2. *PC-oriented.* This category contains publications whose readers straddle the line between being end-users and computer professionals, given the preponderance of PC usage among non-computer-types. Product-oriented articles, technology tutorials, and similar articles are appropriate to submit to these types of periodicals.

3. *Product-specific.* This category can be viewed as a subset of either of the first two categories, and primarily the PC-oriented periodicals. Most of the popular computer systems have had or still have publications dedicated to their products. Articles that contain usage tips and similar product-specific subjects might target these publications, such as *MacWorld.*

4. *Technology-specific.* Many of the leading technologies, such as database systems and communications, have periodicals dedicated to them. For example, *DBMS* and *Database Programming and Design* are two magazines that deal primarily with database issues. An article about database performance tuning could be submitted to either of these publications.

5. *Company-specific.* The product-oriented category deals primarily with PC-level products. Large companies with many users, such as

1. General

2. PC-Oriented

3. Product-Specific

4. Technology-Specific

5. Company-Specific

Figure 10.2 Categories of computer periodicals.

Digital Equipment Corporation, have third-party magazines dedicated to issues on that company and its products. For example, Digital Equipment is covered in at least three periodicals, all from outside publishers: *DEC Professional, Digital Review,* and *Digital News.* An article that deals specifically with a company's hardware or software would be appropriate for one of these, or a similar publication.

As we mentioned earlier in this chapter, you might also find publishing success in periodicals outside the computer field. General business magazines, airline magazines, personal finance, and other categories of publications often publish technical articles. Be aware, though, that articles likely to be of interest to one of these types of publications should be of a more general nature (example: a survey of laptop computers, or how open systems will affect hardware purchase decisions), rather than an article about technical trends in object-oriented languages.

Correspondingly, technical journals usually are published by and managed through a sponsoring organization, such as the Association for Computing Machinery (ACM) or the Institute of Electrical and Electronic Engineers (IEEE) or a similar group. Within each organization, there are usually several journals, each dedicated to a different technology or discipline, plus a "flagship" journal. Technical papers can be oriented to an applicable journal.

An interesting thing to note is that the lead time for journal publication of a paper often can be several years, given the various editorial policies of technical reviews and other actions. It is not uncommon to see a paper published that was written two or three years prior to the publication date, on a subject that has been superseded by further advances in a particular technology or discipline.

Correspondingly, book publishers can also be divided into several different categories, each for a different kind of writing. Some emphasize textbooks, while others emphasize trade books intended for bookstore sale. Some specialize in specific technologies or categories of products (many leading software firms have their own publishing arms or have alliances with other publishers), while others emphasize either current or future computer technologies, but not both. It pays to check the publication policy of various publishers before submitting proposals (discussed next).

Proposals, Query Letters, and Outlines

Most books about professional writing provide detailed guidance on the process of developing a query letter (a form of a business letter, as discussed in the next chapter), a proposal, and an outline. For the sake of space, we'll summarize some of the major points with respect to this process and provide an example of a query letter and proposal that led to a published book. For further information and examples, you might want to consult a general book about writing.

Proposals for computer books and articles, regardless of how technical the subject matter is, should always be oriented to the *commercial* applicability of the subject matter. That is, will a book about your subject be a success in the marketplace? Will the title of your article on the cover of a magazine sell copies? A proposal should contain, at a minimum:

1. The title of your article and book, along with a brief summary of the contents

2. Why this article or book is needed in the marketplace

3. Who your target audience is (programmers, analysts, managers, and so on)

4. (More applicable for books) why your book will be a successful

5. Your qualifications for writing the book or article, such as extensive experience with the product or technology about which you are writing. More importantly, if you can state it, why you are the person who should write this book

6. Competition, such as other books or articles in other magazines, and how your writing is different from *and better* than any preexisting writing on the subject matter

A general rule of thumb, but one that should be examined case-by-case, is that book proposals should be accompanied by an outline, while article proposals may be accompanied by an outline if the article has not yet been written, or by the article itself if completed. It is best to verify the submission policy of each publisher, which will also let you know if simultaneous submissions (with another publisher) are acceptable as well as other information.

At the end of this chapter are the query letter, the proposal, and the outline for a previous book (and companion volume) one of the authors wrote. As you will see, the proposal clearly specifies the commercial potential of the book, information of paramount importance to most publishers.

Guidelines for Writing

Before we leave the subject of professional writing and take a quick look at a sample proposal package, let's discuss some guidelines that can make the difference if your goal is *successful* and *continued* writing.

1. *Write what you know.* If your areas of expertise are distributed databases, open systems, CASE, or some other area, concentrate on

those subject areas, particularly during your initial publishing attempts. It is often easier to develop a winning proposal and convince a publisher that your work should be published if you concentrate on areas in which you are the most comfortable.

2. *Write in an appropriate style.* By this, we mean that your writing style should be determined by the target audience and the type of book you are writing. More importantly, your own background and experiences will influence such a decision. For example, if you are writing a book about distributed databases, your writing style will vary according to these factors, as shown below.

Intended audience	Type of book	Writing style
Academic/computer science	Textbook	Many algorithms and proofs; patterned after a technical paper
MIS managers	Handbook	Tutorial, explanatory in nature; possibly contain discussions of commercial products
Software consultants	Product-specific trade book	Will contain a feature-by-feature discussion of the distributed database product

Note that the type of book you write, and thus the style in which you write, is often dictated by your own background. If you are a computer science professor, you might feel most comfortable writing a textbook, and in turn receive the most career benefit from that form. If, however, you are attempting to build a consulting practice around distributed databases, either of the latter two above may be more applicable to your career and you might feel more comfortable with one of them.

3. *Find niches and combinations of topics.* It is often advisable to find certain niche areas which are sparsely covered, or not covered at all, in existing books, magazine articles, and/or technical papers. The first book one of the authors wrote, *How to Be a Successful Computer Consultant* (McGraw-Hill, 1985, 1990), was written while building a consulting practice, and information had to be gathered from numerous sources. The need for a single comprehensive source of material on starting a computer consulting business led to the marketability and acceptance of that book.

Sometimes the uniqueness of a book or article may come from combinations of subjects. For example, a book on COBOL in open systems environments may be unique in the marketplace, and if it is deemed that such a book can be successfully marketed and sold, it may be a winner.

4. *Diversify across subjects and classes, once established.* While we wrote above that you should concentrate on areas with which you are

familiar, it does pay to diversify as much as possible as your writing career progresses. If you are writing books and articles about database design and data modeling, you may consider writing about CASE, given the automated data modeling tools within CASE.

5. *Use coauthors for splitting of work and adding expertise.* At times (such as during the writing of this particular book) a combination of authors may provide a great deal of synergy to allow for other work or to add particular areas of expertise.

6. *Don't be afraid to go for the "big stuff"—books—before articles.* The traditional writing model is to write articles and technical papers for a while before attempting to write a book. The above-referenced book on computer consulting by one of the authors was proposed and accepted without any professional writing experience in articles or papers. Your target form of expression should be dictated by whether you believe you could develop a successful article or book, based on the amount of material, your available time, and other factors, rather than some stereotyped pattern of writing.

7. *Try to achieve synergy between your writing efforts.* In addition to diversifying your writing efforts, you should try to "piggyback" efforts on one another if you believe that you can create a "package" of your work. For example, two works of one of the authors—the above-mentioned consulting book and *The Computer Professional's Survival Guide* (the query letter, proposal, and outline for which are reproduced at the end of this chapter)—are closely related to this book in that all three deal with career-oriented computer topics rather than technology.

Summary

This chapter has diverged a bit from the subject matter of the earlier chapters, but in a direction that can be extremely helpful to your career. We wish to emphasize again a very important point: The computer profession has changed dramatically in the past several years, and professionals in the field face a tightening job market, increased career stagnation, and other problems that were impossible to imagine just a few years ago. Professional quality writing can often give an edge to your qualifications, and to your resume, which often can make the difference in employment opportunities, promotions, and contract awards.

Sample Query Letter, Book Proposal, and Book Outline

Alan R. Simon
555 Waters Lane
Colorado Springs, CO 80000
(719) 555-0000

March 21, 1990

Ms. Jeanne Glasser
McGraw-Hill, Inc.
Professional Book Group
11 West 19th Street
New York, NY 10011

Dear Ms. Glasser,

Attached please find a proposal and an outline for a book entitled

The Computer Professional's Survival Guide

I believe that this book will be a valuable and profitable addition
to McGraw-Hill's Professional Book Group offerings, and I look forward to any comments or suggestions you may have.

Sincerely,

Alan R. Simon

Attachments: Proposal and Outline

Proposal for
The Computer Professional's Survival Guide

Concept

The purpose of *The Computer Professional's Survival Guide* is to provide a comprehensive and consolidated reference source for various aspects of computer careers, such as educational alternatives, career paths, related careers, and self-help for the reader.

Too many entry-level computer professionals, as well as the hundreds of thousands of high school and college students considering a computer career, don't understand the difference between, for example, a computer science career in developing operating system driver routines and one in developing information systems emphasizing CASE tools and fourth-generation language (4GL). To many people considering the career field, the term "computer career" still signifies "computer programming." Even in the area of programming, there are vast differences between the skills and backgrounds required to write compilers, and those required to develop financial or business applications.

The Computer Professional's Survival Guide is designed not only to provide a reference source for those already in the career field, but to help those people considering a computer-related career *before* they choose a course of study or training. If someone is better suited to developing business applications using 4GLs and CASE tools rather than operating systems internals or compilers, it is best to know that before beginning college training. Nearly 16 years ago I was in this same situation, and almost chose a computer engineering curriculum, for which I had little aptitude, rather than one on business-oriented information systems. At the time, I didn't understand the vast differences between the two.

I believe that *The Computer Professional's Survival Guide* can be marketed successfully as "the indispensable guide to planning a computer career into the next century."

Experience Base for Writing this Book

In my years in the computer career field, I have worked in a number of different capacities, including computer consulting, computer business management, systems programming, applications development, and teaching. I've worked for federal and state governmental agencies, large computer vendors, small consulting companies, universities, and have run my own businesses. In addition to the areas with which I have had personal experience, I have also worked closely with hardware engineers, supercomputer specialists, and others from nearly every area of the computer career field. I feel as qualified as anyone to explain, in clear, understandable language, the differences, advantages, and disadvantages of potential career paths. I have counseled many people with whom I have worked, or who were students of mine, on these exact same topics; what has convinced me that this book is highly marketable is the lack of clear knowledge that still exists even among people in the career field.

Finally, I intend to supplement my own experience with extensive research and interviews with a number of companies and organizations to substantiate and enhance the book's contents.

Outline*

Note: Each chapter will include several brief case studies/inserts, each approximately ¾ page, that will highlight the textual material. For example, Chap. 3 will have a brief case study on "working as an agency recruiter," featuring a brief interview with someone from Source EDP, Robert Half, or a similar firm. The case study will discuss the educational background, career path (past and future), working environment, and other relevant information for that person's position.

The interviews will be spaced in the most appropriate place among the various chapters based on that chapter's material and what that particular person/position stresses (education, career path, etc.).

Chapter 1   An Overview of the Computer Career Field (est. 15–20 pages)

This chapter will preview the contents of the rest of the book, including:

- Different computer positions (software development; systems analysis; hardware engineering; systems integration; etc.) and how computer career paths are different today than they were even 10 years ago. Based on reviewer comments, this section will emphasize this information, based on job function (software development, for example, rather than "programming" or "software engineering") and stress that one organization's "software engineer" may perform identical functions to another's "software architect," or another company's "quality assurance tester."

*In the interest of space we have included only the detailed outline for several of the chapters rather than the entire book.

- Different educational programs at various levels (undergraduate and graduate) and how educational paths and decisions are important to one's career, both in the initial stages and during latter phases.

- Emphasis that not everyone is suited for "just any computer job"; a person with a business-oriented aptitude and an engineering-oriented one both can succeed in the career field in different areas. This may be one of the book's most valuable contributions, since I have observed that many people in the field are frustrated by what they are doing because they are far more suited for an entirely different role within the computer field. Computer professionals can use the information in this book to maximize their career potential by matching the types of positions, career paths, organizational environments, and technology areas with their own backgrounds and interests.

Chapter 2   Surviving and Thriving in Turbulent Times *(est. 25 pages)*

Topics include:

- The computer career climate of the early 1990s:

  Downsizing (voluntary severances, layoffs)

  Outsourcing

  Mergers and acquisitions (especially foreign-owned ones)

  User industry slumps (financial services, real estate, etc.)

  Technology shifts

  　Enterprise architectures (SAA, NAS)

  　Operating system and open architectural shifts (UNIX, OSI, etc.)

  　Downsizing of mainframes into server sets

- How to prepare for possible career uprooting

  Detect above trends early; recognize danger signs in company's industry, computer industry as a whole, general economy, and one's technical areas

- Actions to take (detailed throughout rest of the book)

  Education and training into new technology areas; specifically areas of interest or problem areas for one's organization

  Become the expert in new technology areas (example: what I did with personal computers in the Air Force, despite the mainframe environment at the time)

Keep up at least a semi-active job search; periodically interview or at least look at what's available, keep abreast of salaries, etc.

Personal side: try to build personal savings, scale down personal debt, be prepared for the worst

Moonlighting; contract programming, consulting, writing (references to *How to Be a Successful Computer Consultant*)

- Options if the reader is affected by downsizing, layoffs, etc.:

Move to the outsourcer (example: Kodak employees absorbed by Digital)

Go into solo work (consulting, contract)

Look for a new career position; may be tough in some geographical areas

Others (using case studies and examples)

Chapter 3   Computer Positions and Careers
(est. 60 pages; may be divided into multiple chapters if too unwieldy)

This chapter will discuss the different types of computer career positions available. For each position, a number of different factors and items will be discussed, including:

- Educational background
- Aptitudes
- Job functions
- Typical career paths (Chap. 4 discusses career paths in more detail; this chapter will briefly discuss the topic respective to each position)
- Advantages and disadvantages of the explicit job and its career path (for example, systems programming is on the downside, but there still are positions for those interested)
- Compensation and salaries (relative to other computer positions)
- Other applicable information

Positions to be discussed include:

1. *Software development.* This is the largest category, and includes job titles such as programing, software development professional, and software engineer. Positions almost always involve coding.

- Applications (business; scientific; engineering; other)

  New systems development

  Software maintenance (tedious, but necessary, especially in large organizations)

- Systems (compiler, operating systems, tools and utilities; other)

  Not as lucrative in recent years, as portable operating systems and environments (DOS, UNIX) decrease the number of people writing operating systems kernels and device drivers; however, there are still many positions and career paths, mostly at major vendors

- Real-time computer graphics programmer

  Writing video game software

  Movie industry computer graphics (a growing specialty area)

- Integration (specializing in integrating other commercial and/or custom software)

  Requires knowledge of emerging information architectures such as IBM's SAA, Digital's NAS, HP's New Wave, etc.

- Technical specialties (i.e. telecommunications programmer; database applications programmer; CASE or 4GL-based applications generation; other)

  Emphasis point here: there is a big difference between a software developer doing IMS and COBOL maintenance in an IBM mainframe environment and one developing new client-server, workstation-based database applications. This portion will be a lead-in to Chap. 7 (Hot Technology Areas) by discussing how to tailor one's career, *if desired,* towards emerging and lucrative technologies

- Programming user interfaces, such as X-Windows or DECWindows

- Specialist in prototyping applications and environments

- Positions in software testing, quality assurance, and other areas of the development life cycle.

2. *Systems analyst.* Usually noncoding positions; applications-oriented; geared towards gathering requirements and providing initial specifications and architectures. *There still are systems analysis positions, especially in large corporations, that are not lumped together with software development as defined above.*

- Business requirements analyst, doing initial requirements and feasibility analysis
- Specialist in designing user interfaces, working closely with users
- Specialist in writing code specifications, interfaces with "pure coders," which also still exist

3. *Supervisory and management positions.*

- Software development supervisor: first line above developers, usually involved with planning, staffing, resource requests, scheduling and tracking
- Software development manager: often manages several development efforts; attempts to coordinate efforts and schedules; usually involved in politically oriented negotiations re: staff levels, resource allocations, etc.
- Product manager: coordinates development, training, field testing, marketing, and product introduction products, usually for vendors
- Senior management positions
  Chief information officer
  President or Vice President at vendor
  Other vendor senior management

4. *Consultant (including "internal consultants").* Information adapted from my consulting book

5. *Sales positions.* Usually at vendors; often commission-based compensation; how to find a lucrative sales position

6. *Hardware engineering.* Peripherals, CPUs, etc.; just as with systems programming is a shrinking base due to standardized peripherals, processors, and memory, but still are positions, particularly in new or research-oriented areas (massively parallel processor systems; neural network systems; optical storage devices)

7. *Data analyst.*

8. *Technical writing.*

- Documentation specialist
- Commercial (computer periodical) writer

9. *Recruiting and personnel.* Corporate personnel (in computer field) is on downside as large vendors release many people, but recruiting firms ("headhunters") is still a good field as job-hopping continues

10. *Data communications and telecommunications.* While the merging of computer and communication technology will continue, there are still communication-specific positions that don't involve software development or "traditional computing," such as strapping communications boards and designing and installing cable plants. This section will discuss these positions as well as those which are oriented towards computing, such as communications programming, LAN configuration, etc.

11. *Computer operations.* Also on the downswing, but large mainframe-based organizations (Government and corporate) still have a need for operations managers.

12. *Teaching.*

   - University or college: Full-time tenure track as well as part-time; environments; importance of teaching and research; ability to perform outside activities such as consulting; how to balance part-time teaching with one's primary career position
   - Company trainer

Chapter 4   Companies, Organizations, and Environments *(est. 40 pages)*

This chapter will discuss the number of different, *overlapping* ways in which one's career environment can be categorized. These classification areas include, at a minimum:

Classification 1: *Types of organization*

   - Commercial "users of systems" (a *Fortune* 500 manufacturing company, for example); these firms are *users,* not producers, of information systems; they are profit-driven; information technology may be secondary within these organizations to the business line functions, which may be career-limiting
   - Commercial developers of systems (vendors); distinction from above: information technology *is* the line of business; including hardware/software vendors (IBM, Digital), software vendors (Informix, Oracle), and service-oriented (Big 6 consulting firm, systems integrators such as EDS, custom software firms); distinctions between product-oriented firms and service-oriented ones
   - Government "users of systems"; similar to commercial users, but not profit-driven; the distinctions and tradeoffs between Government and commercial organizations

- Nonprofit organizations; small category, and discussed only briefly

Classification 2: *Environment*

- Development-oriented

  Usually uses proven technology

  Geared towards specific results

  May include maintenance and other life-cycle (QA, for example) functions

  Life-cycle oriented

- Research

  Different levels, from proof-of-concept development (example: IBM's System R and Starburst relational database projects) to "forefront of technology" (neural networks, for example) research

  Often diverges from initial goals

  Sometimes in large organizations (IBM)

  Research consortiums (Software Engineering Institute; Software Productivity Consortium; Sematech; etc.)

  Fuzzier than development-oriented environment; *the definitions of success, and the reward structure,* is different from development

  University-based research; geared towards student development as well as reputation and attracting funds

Classification 3: *Levels of technology*

- State-of-the art environments (workstations, LANs, object-oriented databases, CASE tools), versus

- "Old technology" environments (IBM mainframes; IMS; COBOL; batch remote job entry); many environments are still this way, and it is *not necessarily* a career-limiter for someone to learn "old technology" especially if they wish to eventually integrate new technology into old environments

The chapter will discuss which environments are best suited for "fast track" computer professionals; relative degrees of security; typical compensation packages (including bonuses and educational benefits); and different working environments (having one's own workstation versus timesharing on an IBM mainframe, for example). Tradeoffs such as working regular 40-hour weeks in most Government jobs but being limited in pay and promotion are also discussed.

11

Writing Effective Business Letters

Business letters are communications. As we will discuss in the chapters that follow, verbal communications (Chap. 12) and presentations (Chap. 13) attempt to establish a communication relationship. However, unlike face-to-face interactions where you can receive visual feedback and discern whether your message is being comprehended in the manner intended, you only have one chance with a business letter. Since your letter represents your skills and thoughts, ultimately it represents you.

Business writers often fall into two categories: those who are intimidated by writing, and those who write just by transferring the words from their minds to their hands. Both types of writers are dangerous in that they inhibit effective business writing. Volumes have been written about business writing. Accordingly, this chapter is designed to give you a brief overview of what an effective business letter is, why it is important, and a few examples of business letters.

Effective Business Letters

First let us examine what business letters are not. They are not essays or short stories, with descriptive adjectives and extensive background information. Why? Because in most cases, your audience or reader has limited time. Therefore, brevity is the key. As an example, if you are a product manager, your letter may be a follow-up to your presentation. Your job is to briefly highlight what you need to say, and if appropriate ask for your reader's course of action.

Another common form of written correspondence is the memorandum (memo). Memos are used most often internally; that is, within a company. They are an abbreviated form of written communication intended to provide the reader with a brief overview of the subject matter. The distinguishing component of the memo is its informality; it is a less formal means of communication than the business letter. The sample memo at the end of this chapter highlights the difference between a memo and a business letter.

Many letter writing books, including this one, provide you with a series of steps to employ in the letter-writing process. Whichever procedure you use, the most important thing to keep in mind is why you are writing the business letter and what you want it to accomplish. If you never lose sight of these two important points while writing, your business letter will be effective. Is the letter intended to call to mind a recent meeting with a new customer about a software installation? Is it a contact letter for a desired meeting? Or is it to reiterate the reasons your client should proceed with your recommended systems installation after you have presented it to the company? Whatever the reason, keep focusing on why you are writing the letter and what you want it to accomplish.

It is all too easy to forget how your business letters can shape your reader's opinion of you. Your letter represents you, and thus it directly reflects on your ability as a computer professional. It should positively reinforce your reader's image of both you and your computer abilities; correspondence that does not project a positive image of you could cost you business. Your verbal communication and presentation skills may be highly professional and dynamic, but written communication skills are the hard-copy component of the communication relationship.

Writing Business Letters

As with other forms of communication, a systematic approach is often the key. Five basic steps are often used in business writing.[1] These five steps are preparation, research, organization, draft writing, and revision. A major component of effective business writing is your ability to be flexible and to key each letter to the specific business situation. The time you spend on each of the steps may vary, depending on the letter you are writing, and the actual writing does not begin until the fourth step. This highlights the importance of preparatory work in business writing. Preparation, research, and organization should include asking yourself, "What do I want this letter to accomplish?" As mentioned above, your ability to focus on this question while preparing to write your letter will enable you to build the foundation of an effective business letter. The following passages provide a brief overview of the five steps to effective business writing.

Preparation

Preparation is your opportunity to establish your objective. This is the answer to, "What do I want this letter to accomplish," and to identify your reader. As we will discuss in later chapters, it is crucial that you gather as much information as possible about your audience or reader prior to the actual communication. The business letter will be effective only if it hits your target audience. Your chances of effectively reaching your reader are greatly enhanced by researching the reader prior to the actual letter-writing. Have you talked with the reader beforehand, or is this the first communication? What is your reader's computer level of knowledge on the subject matter?

It may not be appropriate to discuss obvious, basic points in your letter. Conversely, there may be occasions when it is appropriate and even necessary to highlight these points. This decision calls into play your writing flexibility. Tailor each letter to the specific situation. Preparation helps you decide what to say or what not say in your letter.

Research

Research is the next logical step after the preparation phase. It is your opportunity to gather as much as information as you need from sources that help you form the basis of your letter. Your sources may come from various places, including libraries, books, magazines, personal interviews, and your own knowledge. Once again, focus on the objective of your letter while performing your research. Do not waste time on unnecessary research, but make sure that you have gathered enough information for your letter. The length of time spent on this phase of your letter writing is determined by its subject matter. A letter highlighting last week's meeting with your client on new software involves little research, whereas a letter attempting to gain an audience with the board of directors to discuss the company's need for a new computer system involves more.

Organization

This step in the writing process involves gathering the various individual "bytes" of data and information you have obtained in the preparation and research steps, and molding them into an organized sequence. It is not the point at which a rough draft should be written. Rather, it is the point at which you classify your information into related subject matter. If you have gathered information from a variety of sources, this is your opportunity to organize it to determine if you have all of the necessary components to proceed with your letter writing. Unless you are a proficient, experienced writer, do not skip this step.

Draft Writing

Most of us would like to be able to sit at our computer and type the letter in first and final form. In reality, very few people can do this. Consequently, draft writing can be the most frustrating step in writing a letter. The key here is to write down your ideas in a clear, concise, and organized manner. Your reader must know the reason (your objective) for writing the letter in the first few sentences. This serves a dual purpose: It lets your reader know what you will be discussing and simultaneously forces your reader to focus in on the subject matter.

The body of your letter should state clearly the points you wish to discuss. Short paragraphs are visually appealing to the business reader, who may skim or completely skip a paragraph that is too long. Unfortunately, the portion the reader skipped probably contains important information he or she should be digesting. So keep your paragraphs short.

The letter should conclude with a relevant closing. As an example, if you are asking for a follow-up meeting, say so, and suggest a date and time. If you are asking a client to take a specific course of action, clearly state what it is and provide a time frame. You do not want to leave any doubt in the reader's mind about his or her response to your communication. Remember, the letter is establishing a communication relationship; you must clearly guide the relationship to the intended next stage.

Revision

The revision process involves self-critique. As we will discuss in Chap. 13, "Presentations," this stage forces you to step back and analyze your communication, in this case your letter, through the eyes of the reader. Does your letter clearly state your points? Read it as though for the first time, pretending you are the recipient and not the author.

Your letter should have an overall tone and unity of style. The transitions between paragraphs should flow logically as your points in the letter unfold. Though it may seem obvious, do not forget to check your grammar, spelling, and punctuation. Nothing is more counterproductive to a professionally written business letter than a misspelled word. It detracts your reader's focus from the letter's contents.

The final product should be a communication you feel confident in sending. Speaking of confidence, it is the one skill in writing that is the hardest to attain. You have the credibility, an essential element in the communication process discussed in Chap. 13, by virtue of your education and background. The best way to gain confidence in your writing ability is to practice. It may be helpful to write a few standard templates for letters that you think you will use frequently. However, remember that the hallmark of the effective business letter is its uniqueness to the specific business situation.

Examples

The following are examples of business letters and memorandums that a computer professional may encounter in the course of business. Each communication is explained in terms of a specific business scenario.

Sample detailed business letter

This business letter is intended to summarize the contractor use status for M. McCauley Corporation's purchase of new inventory management software. Tom Pothoff, the acquisitions manager hired by M. McCauley Corporation, is attempting to highlight the current status to Carol Carter, the project supervisor for the software installation.

You should note that business letters that summarize meetings serve a dual purpose: They provide a written record of what the parties previously agreed to, and they help to avoid future problems and discrepancies.

June 5, 1992

Ms. Carol Carter
2983 Lexington Way
Tucson, AZ 85715

Dear Ms. Carter:

This letter summarizes our status review meeting of May 28, 1992, for the M. McCauley Corporation inventory management software project. While I am pleased with the general contract status, there are several items of concern:

1. After our last meeting, it became apparent that Phase II of this project is currently two month's behind schedule as a result of hardware acquisition problems. I recognize that these problems are beyond your control. However, I do want to confirm, per our initial meeting,

that the backup hardware system can be implemented on a timely basis. Perhaps it is time to consider this measure.

2. The live test demonstration (LTD) on May 20, 1992, was satisfactory overall. I am concerned, however, about the locking capabilities of the inventory database. At the LTD demonstration, I brought this concern to your attention, and you assured me that this will be resolved at the time of installation.

3. As demonstrated at the LTD, as of this date the user interface (UI) software is an unreleased, unsupported package from the vendor. I have been assured by your associate, Greg Yost, that at installation time the UI software will be an announced, supported package.

4. As a reminder, the inventory management system must be retrofitted and integrated with the general ledger and accounts payable system that M. McCauley Corporation currently uses. This was supposed to be demonstrated at the LTD but was unavailable. Once again, you have assured me that this will be available at installation time.

5. I am concerned about the loss of personnel assigned to this project. This is to confirm your promise to find adequate personnel replacements for this project.

I am pleased with the overall progress on this project. The company believes that a good working relationship between us exists. I look forward to the next LTD, scheduled for August 10, 1992.

Sincerely,

Tom Pothoff

cc: J. Kelly Robinson, M. McCauley Corporation
     Frances Libby, M. McCauley Corporation

Sample confirmation business letter

This business letter is a confirmation of a scheduled meeting. Kathy Zimmermann, a product manager for Kalfas Corporation, is interested in obtaining permission to use a product owned or controlled by the Humphrey Software Corporation. She has already placed an inquiry phone call to Blake Gillett, a product manager for Humphrey.

The letter should be brief and to the point. Its objective is to provide Gillett with a brief summary of their conversation and to confirm the meeting.

July 25, 1992

Mr. Blake Gillett
Humphrey Software Corporation
10456 Williamsburg Avenue
Mountaintop, PA 18706

Dear Mr. Gillett:

I enjoyed our recent conversation regarding our licensing of your repository backplane to use in our CASE environment. As we discussed, Kalfas Corporation believes that there is a synergy between your backplane product and our integrated set of CASE tools.

I look forward to meeting with you on Friday, August 7, 1992, at 10:00 a.m. at your office to discuss this licensing. If you have any questions, please contact me at (415) 555-6151.

Sincerely,

Kathy Zimmermann

Sample memorandum

As previously mentioned in this chapter, memorandums are a less formal means of communication than most other types of business correspondence. They are often used within a corporation. This example is an electronic mail (E-mail) memo. Corporations that use E-mail often overload their employees with it. Therefore, when sending an E-mail memo, remember to be succinct and brief.

In our example, Jack Sevey, a software development manager at a Fortune 100 company, is sending an E-mail memo to the legal department inquiring about a trademark search.

From: Jack Sevey, Software Development Manager
To: Brian Lee and Kevin Wilson, Trademark Attorneys,
          Language Development
Subject: Status of trademark search
Date: August 11, 1992

I am inquiring about the status of the trademark search for the source code management system. As a reminder, we are due to close on Phase 1 of development on September 22, 1992, and we need to have chosen a name by then.

Please inform me of the status of candidate names previously sent to you.

Thank you for your prompt attention in this matter.

Reference: E-mail message of July 6, 1992

Summary

Business letters are more than forms of communication. They should be viewed as opportunities to showcase your written communication skills, which ultimately showcase your computer skills. Throughout the five-step writing process discussed, the purpose of your correspondence, whether a formal business letter or an informal internal memorandum, should guide your writing process. Your ability to keep your focus on the main objective of your correspondence will enable you to communicate effectively with your intended audience. Remember, each business letter or memorandum must be tailored to the specific business situation.

The various types of business letters range from brief confirmation letters to detailed summaries. Your letter's effectiveness is enhanced by your awareness of your reader's knowledge of the subject matter (acquired through the first step, in the letter-writing process, preparation); proper research (step 2); and organization. The cumulative information from this background work will provide the foundation for a draft of your correspondence. Once again, the time you spend on the various steps in the writing process depends on the type of correspondence in which you are engaged.

Informal memorandums normally require little preparation before you write your draft, and you may be able to revise your memo at the same time as you draft it; a detailed business letter, however, will probably require time spent on the preparatory steps of the process. As in all business situations, be flexible, and adapt your letter and the amount of time you spend on it to the particular scenario.

The ability to correlate your written communication skills to a particular business situation will help you to communicate effectively. This will be a significant step in establishing a communication relationship. Once you feel comfortable communicating in writing, it is time to turn your attention to another important component of the communication relationship: verbal communication.

End Note

1. C. T. Brusaw, G. J. Alred, and W. E. Oliu, *The Business Writer's Handbook,* 3d ed., St. Martin's Press, New York, 1987.

2

Effective Verbal Communication Skills for the Computer Field

Chapter

12

Overview of
Verbal Communications

Lalophobia is the average person's most often cited fear. Lalophobia, defined as the irrational fear of speaking,[1] is derived from the Greek word "lalein," which means to babble. Unfortunately, "babble" is often the appropriate word for people—including many computer professionals—when they think about public speaking. Though by definition a phobia is irrational, it is a very real phenomenon that many of us have some time experienced. Most of us can remember with discomfort the high school or college experience that required us to speak publicly; those were the times that writing a fifty-page paper seemed more and more appealing. Why do we have this fear? It is because most of us never learned the fundamentals of communication; communication is more than the words we say. It is an equation consisting of two inseparable components—verbal and nonverbal communication, the end products of the communication process. However, the most basic, underlying part of communication is the one we often fail to recognize and because of that, often fail to achieve: Communication is the creation of a relationship.

Verbal Communication

Verbal communication is more than the words you say; it is the end product. How that end product can achieve the desired result is our main concern when we discuss verbal communication.

Words are the most powerful medium of expression human beings have. While "actions speak louder than words," the initial phase of most business interactions for computer professionals is verbal-based.

First impressions are the result of another person's opinion of your verbal skills. Consequently, sharpening these skills is crucial to selling yourself and your services.

Verbal communication comprises many different elements: intonation, pitch, tone, enunciation, and verbiage. Intonation, pitch, and tone are the instruments your voice uses to create and convey meaning to your words. Our voices convey our emotions more than we realize. For example, an enthusiastic tone can convey a different meaning than the same words spoken lethargically. Your voice can convey confidence or lack of it. Remember, your voice is your calling card to the outside world.

The next time you watch television, notice how the volume increases when a commercial begins. This is not because the sound engineer forgot to adjust the volume control. It is the advertiser's way of grabbing your attention. Initially grabbing your audience's attention may not be difficult. But retaining its undivided attention is often another story.

One of the most common mistakes public speakers make is speaking in a monotonous voice. The *tone* of your voice is the quality of its sound. Remember, although you may be saying something for the hundredth time, it is the first time your audience has heard it. Your words will not be heard, let alone comprehended, if you do not constantly, though subtly, change your voice's pitch and tone. To achieve the desired effect these "breaks" in tone should be placed at appropriate transitions in your presentation. Logical places for these voice breaks are achieved by "blocking," a presentation skill examined in Chap. 13.

A word of caution: do not "break" with the word "um." When a speaker finds a natural transition period while speaking, it is a common habit to unconsciously say "um," which is very distracting to your audience. Unfortunately, it is so common that people who must listen to communications littered with "ums" often have contests to see who can count the most "ums" in the speech. It is acceptable and desirable to pause or break and not say anything.

"Enunciation" is the articulation of words. Not enough attention is paid to clear enunciation. The children's game of "telephone," where one child whispers something to the next, who in turn continues this process, until the last child recites aloud what he or she has heard, is an example of the relationship between enunciation and comprehension. The object of this game is to see how different the final message is from the original statement. What happens to that message? The hearers probably do not hear all of the words clearly because they were enunciated poorly. Precise, clear enunciation is essential if the receiver is to hear and comprehend your message.

"Verbiage" is the choice of words. The key here is to match your words to your audience. Whom you are speaking to should determine your choice of words. Consequently, what worked once may need to be refined or revised for a different audience. Another communication trap occurs in this area. A presentation replete with words you found in a thesaurus may sound impressive, but if those words make your audience feel that they need a dictionary to comprehend your message, you have failed to communicate. The idea here is comprehension, not confusion.

We have examined half of the communication equation. If we conceive of verbal communication as an island, nonverbal communication is the water surrounding it.

Nonverbal Communication

Nonverbal communication is the "how you say it" part of the communication equation. Your body language makes its own statement while you are communicating verbally. Obviously, it is important that the verbal and nonverbal statements convey the same message. If they do, your verbal statement is reinforced because your audience receives audiovisual confirmation of it. If the nonverbal communication conveys a different message, doubt is created in the receiver's mind because of the conflicting messages. The goal here is for the receiver to achieve an audiovisual message, *audio* representing verbal and *visual* representing nonverbal communication, where each component complements the other.

Nonverbal communication consists of a variety of body language elements. Your posture conveys more than just how you stand; it tells your audience how you feel. Slouching or rounding your shoulders may be interpreted as a sign of weariness or boredom. When you stand erect with your feet firmly planted, you exude confidence.

A common concern of speakers is what to do with their hands. There is no one answer to this question; it depends on what you normally do with your hands when you speak in a relaxed setting. If you do not normally gesture with your hands, don't attempt to use your hands as a communication device when you make a presentation. If you *do* use your hands when casually speaking, be aware of this fact and use them to emphasize important points in your presentation. Though this can be useful, be careful that your hands do not become deadly weapons. Hand motions should complement, not detract from your verbal communication. Remember, a presentation on computers is not a cooking demonstration. If your audience is too busy watching your hands fly around, your message will be lost before you utter a word.

Facial expressions are another opportunity to dispel doubts your audience may have about your verbal and nonverbal statements. A smile, raised eyebrow, or serious expression to emphasize a point, reinforces the meaning of your words.

One of the most important nonverbal communication skills is the use of eye contact. This skill is often ignored when making large group presentations, because the speaker mistakenly assumes that it is not possible to achieve eye contact with a large audience. Whether your audience is one or a hundred, eye contact is crucial to the "how you say it" part of the communication equation. It is easy to establish eye contact in a relatively small group. In surveying your audience, you make a sweep of their eyes. The next step is to actually focus on one person's eyes for no more than a few seconds. You do not want anyone to feel uncomfortable. Yet, the initial eye contact establishes a visual bond that sparks that person's interest in your communication. Even in large audiences, frequently sweep the room with your eyes. Though you may not actually have the opportunity to establish a visual bond, you create the illusion of a bond with someone in the audience.

Nonverbal communication skills thus can strengthen your verbal communication skills. But it is the underlying communication relationship that is the foundation of the communication equation.

Communication Relationships

All communication, whether verbal or nonverbal, ultimately is intended to create a relationship. The basic goal of this subconscious game is for each participant to define the relationship. The relationship has equal potentiality. The instant the communication begins, this equality is lost, because the communication relationship is either strengthened or diminished based upon the communication received from others.

Whether we are conscious of it or not, each of us has an expectancy set. We harbor preconceived notions of what the communication will be before a word is uttered. Consequently, what is exchanged through verbal and nonverbal communication reinforces or contradicts the audience's preconceived definitions. This is where we attempt to define our communication relationships.

Two levels of meaning are conveyed to your audience each time you speak. The first meaning is contained in your words; the other is what the words say about the communication relationship. This duality is what can cause uncertainty in verbal communication. The key to making the communication relationship work is to have each of the two levels say the same thing. Once the communication relationship is established, it tends to be resistant to change. Therefore, it is important that early on you set a positive relationship.

Summary

In the following chapters, we will examine presentations and the appropriate accompanying materials in more detail. When reading those chapters, keep in mind the basics of verbal communication discussed in this chapter.

Communication relationships are the outgrowth of the communication equation comprising verbal and nonverbal communication. Verbal communication is your ability to communicate with your audience through the powerful medium of words. But more than the choice of words will communicate your message effectively. How you say these words, including intonation, pitch, and enunciation, is equally important.

Nonverbal communication is another powerful component of communication, and is expressed by your body language. Nonverbal communication skills include eye contact, hand usage while speaking, and facial expression.

The key to establishing effective communication is for both the verbal and nonverbal communication components to convey the same message. Once the listener perceives that the communication equation components are consistent, the communication relationship can be established.

End Note

1. *Dorland's Illustrated Medical Dictionary*, 27th ed., Saunders, Philadelphia, 1988.

Chapter

13

Presentations

Verbal and nonverbal communication, as discussed in Chap. 12, is the foundation of an effective presentation. You want your audience to focus its attention on your presentation, not your communication skills. Your presentation will be carefully analyzed by your audience whose analysis will go beyond the actual content of your presentation to the way your material is presented. Therefore, this chapter is intended to provide you with skills that will enhance your presentation.

Various types of presentations are illustrated, so that you can determine the most appropriate format for the goal of a particular presentation. Whether you are a software engineer, product manager, supervisor, or serve in some other capacity in the computer field, inevitably you will be involved with presentations, from code walkthroughs to customer presentations to internal briefings. The skills and techniques this chapter discusses will help to improve your presentations.

Effective Presentations

What is an effective presentation? One that is clearly organized, engages the audience's attention throughout, provides appropriate explanations and examples, and ultimately gives your audience a memorable, positive experience. Remember, a presentation is equivalent to a sales call. You are attempting to sell yourself and your services. Statistics show that a large proportion of information disseminated during a presentation is never received by the audience to which it is directed. Think of this proportion of lost information as bad bytes on a hard drive; you need to reorchestrate your approach to avoid these misplaced bytes of vital information.

Presentation Strategies

Presentations are communications. Before you begin to organize any presentation, you should step back and rethink it. Presentations are more than segments of information and data; they are a series of *communication strategies* that provide your audience with the information and data you want them to absorb. This is your chance to create the communication relationship discussed in Chap. 12 in the manner you desire. Transforming presentations into strategies is not an easy task; it is tempting to skip this part of your preparation. But, if you want your audience to take the action you want it to, you must take the time to recast the macro presentation into micro strategies. This crucial step in preparing a presentation often is the difference between its success and failure.

The following presentation strategies will provide you with a set of strategic skills to enhance your communication skills. The combination of these communication and presentation strategy skills will be the foundation of a successful presentation.

Attention processing

The average person is bombarded with hundreds of stimuli per minute, but only a small percentage is actually processed by the brain. The key is to not give your audience a chance to selectively decide whether to process the information you are providing. You must grab its attention and eliminate all other interfering, attention-stealing stimuli. If your presentation's topic involves a new software product your company is marketing, you want to ensure that your audience absorbs all of your key marketing messages. A successful attention processing technique will keep your audience's mind on your presentation.

Attention-getting techniques can range from surprising opening statements to computer demonstrations highlighting why your computer skills are needed. Tailor the attention processing to your audience; what worked once may not be as effective in the future. Attention processing is also achieved by your verbal communication, including your language choices. Carefully match your verbiage to your audience. The importance of knowing your audience will be discussed later in this chapter.

Need

A course in psychology often includes the study of Maslow's hierarchy of needs, which classifies human motives in the order of their complexity and importance in satisfying basic human needs. While it would be a stretch to place a presentation at the top-of-the pyramid of self-actualization, a presenter must nonetheless establish need in the audience or listener's mind. To create need, you may use a four-step process, as discussed below:

1. *Problem statement creation.* If it is appropriate in your presentation, begin with a statement outlining the problem. Relate how you and your computer skills can correct the problem. If there are no apparent problems, you can still tone down a "problem" statement to a "need statement" by telling your audience why it needs you and your services. Both types of statements should be clear and concise. It is a sufficient communication challenge to have your audience comprehend all of the information you present; do not confuse them with an unclear problem or need statement at the beginning of the presentation.

2. *Illustration.* Processing information is difficult in and of itself. Human beings process material more effectively and efficiently if they are given examples. Whether your examples are generic or specific, select those to which a particular audience can relate. Carefully chosen illustrations can increase your credibility, an essential element in verbal communication, discussed later in this chapter.

3. *Ramification.* Most adults realize that every action and decision has ramifications. Your job is to give your audience a clear picture of the ramifications of your program after you have established the need. This is the "benefit" part of the "cost/benefit" analysis that your audience may be subconsciously analyzing. Ramifications traditionally are presented as a positive reinforcement or solution to the problem statement. On rare occasions, you may want to present the ramifications as a negative reinforcement of what might happen if the problem you discussed is not corrected. This tactic should be employed sparingly, and only if deemed appropriate because of the nature of the problem. The nature of the ramifications is best established by using illustrations, as discussed in the previous paragraph.

4. *Pointing.* Ramifications are not easily established with your audience. *Pointing,* that is, the prior discovery of the words to show your audience how it will be directly affected, can help that audience understand the ramifications. Discovering the most appropriate words and the format in which to use them are the direct result of your preparatory work. You understand who your audience is and the level of its knowledge. This is another example of how important it is to choose the correct words if you expect to communicate effectively with your audience.

Satisfaction

We have now examined two presentation strategies: *attention and need.* Hopefully, you now have the audience's attention and have established the need in its mind. Where do you go from here? The natural progression is next to provide your audience with *satisfaction*. But before you can provide this satisfaction, you must first meet any questions or concerns your audience has before those concerns are raised. Once questions or concerns are raised, you must be prepared to prevent them from being transformed into doubts and fears. If this should happen, your credibility, discussed later in this chapter, is greatly diminished. The ability to know beforehand what those questions and concerns will be may seem improbable, especially in a presentation to a large audience. The key is to carefully evaluate and critique your own presentation before you give it.

A trial run to a business colleague or your spouse often is advantageous in toning the delivery aspects of a presentation. However, to truly critique your own presentation, you must hear (and see) it not as the presenter, but rather as the audience. The method of choice is to tape yourself on a camcorder. Many people are surprised at what they see and hear. (This is also an effective means of critiquing your basic communication and presentation skills.) If this is not possible, at least critique the audio portion of your presentation by taping it. The audiovisual self-critique will enable you to be proactive, rather than retroactive, in response to your audiences concerns. If you use this technique to anticipate those concerns you will be able to revise your presentation before you make it in front of an audience.

Visualization

Previously we examined the importance of illustration, which we discussed with the presentation strategy of *need*. *Visualization* goes beyond illustration: Illustration is the ability to relate to your audience through examples; *visualization* takes the concept of illustration and expands it beyond the level of examples. It is the ability to articulate the vision you want your audience to comprehend. This vision is a future vision based on the solutions you are presenting. While illustration aids in micro examples, visualization is the macro picture you are striving to have your audience see. This should be a goal of your presentation, because visualization helps your audience transform the individual pieces of data and information into the solution you want to project. Audience visualization is the most difficult to achieve of all the presentation strategies. However, if you have successfully employed the presentation strategies discussed, gained and held your audience's attention, established need, and presented satisfaction, visualization is possible.

Action

The presentation strategy of *action* is important for the presenter to convey to the audience. At this point in your presentation, you have given the audience the facts. The next logical step is to show it the course of action you want it to follow. You must be precise and clear as to what the action is, whether it is to hear a follow-up presentation or to enlist your computer skills. Remember, an effective presentation is not passive; it is interactive with your audience. You want to engage your audience in this interaction, then think about, and ultimately react to your program after your presentation has been given. Ideally, your audience will leave your presentation with a specific course of action in mind. Even if it leaves the room just thinking about your general concepts, your presentation has been effective.

Speech Skills

We have now examined presentation strategies that will enhance your presentation. Another group of skills to improve your presentations may be termed "Speech Skills." The eight speech skills presented are those which will provide you with basic help in verbalizing your speech or presentation.

Audience reference

We discussed briefly, under "Attention Processing," the importance of knowing your audience. The basic questions, "who, what, why, where and when" can start the process of knowing your audience. First and foremost, discover beforehand "who" your audience is. This may seem difficult, especially with a large audience. However, having this information is vital so that you can match your language choices to your audience. At least one contact person probably has helped you set up your presentation; do not be afraid to ask questions about those you will be addressing. Remember, the key here is to correlate the presentation, including your speech skills, with your audience.

The next question to ask yourself is "what," meaning what does my audience want to know. This is a logical follow-up to the question of "who." What your audience wants to know depends on the extent of their computer knowledge and how the information you will be presenting can benefit them.

The "why" question is often considered the easiest to answer; the audience is there to gather information and learn. But the trick here is to step back and ask yourself why the audience is there. Presenting to a corporate-sponsored audience is quite different from presenting to an

audience of individuals who paid for your computer seminar. Therefore, the "why" question may not be as easy to answer if you correctly
analyze your audience.

The "where" question enables you to further examine the "who"
question in reference to your audience. Where is your audience coming
from? This involves attempting to understand the audience's background knowledge and experience in order to correctly tailor your presentation.

The presenter who takes the time to ask, analyze and answer these
questions about the audience creates a strong foundation for a successful presentation before a single word is uttered.

Credibility

Politicians understand the importance of their credibility with their
constituents. When you are a speaker, you must achieve credibility in
order to form a bond with your audience. It is not easily achieved, par-
tially because normally it takes a long time to build. However, you may
not have the luxury of multiple meetings to build credibility with your
audience. Consequently, you must attempt to establish credibility
throughout your presentation.

In Chap. 12, we discussed the importance of projecting confidence
with your voice. Building confidence is a prerequisite to establishing
credibility. Your preparation, including being prepared to answer the
questions the audience may ask, helps you to establish credibility with
your audience. One of the most important reasons to establish credibility was examined briefly with the presentation strategy of satisfaction.
You must meet head-on any doubts and questions your audience may
have before they become real concerns. You achieve this by having
credibility. The presenter who lacks credibility is wasting the audience's time. No matter how great the presenter's other speech skills,
the presentation will be ineffective if a credibility gap exists, creating
skepticism and doubt about what is being presented. One of your goals
as a presenter is to make sure that a credibility gap does not have a
chance to form.

Cuing

A speech or presentation often is presented as a series of related data
and information. It is easy to assume that your audience is following
your presentation. After all, you know what you are saying and you
clearly see the relationship among the segments of your presentation.
It is this assumption that can lead to audience confusion and lack of
comprehension. As the presenter, it is your responsibility to cue your

audience. *Cuing* is the process of informing your audience where your presentation currently is at, where you are leading them, and ultimately where you will leave them. Chapter 13 discussed the importance of retaining the audience's attention. You were provided with ways to achieve this through voice techniques. Cuing employs those voice techniques, as well as actual verbal statements outlining your presentation. If it comes down to a choice between verbalizing the outline of your presentation or losing your audience, the former is preferable. It is hard to retain audience attention without cuing. The lack of it can result in fragmented listening which destroys the communication relationship you have worked hard to establish.

Immediacy effect

Cuing enables the presenter to keep the attention of the audience. However, before you can cue the audience, you first must grab its attention. Psychology terms the *immediacy effect* the *primacy effect,* which studies of impression formation (our communication relationships) describe as the tendency for initial information to carry more weight than information received at a later time.[1] The immediacy effect is a speech skill whereby the presenter hits the audience (figuratively speaking) with something strong and powerful. There are many ways to grab attention: verbal communication techniques such as voice pitch, or beginning the presentation with unexpected presentation materials (discussed in Chap. 15). The immediacy effect does more than get the audience's attention; it helps to establish the communication relationship. As examined in Chap. 12, the communication relationship can be either strengthened or weakened after it has begun. The immediacy effect gets the communication relationship off to a strong start.

Recency effect

The *recency effect* is a speech skill to strengthen the communication relationship by leaving the audience with something memorable. In psychology terminology, it is the opposite of the primacy effect. The recency effect describes the tendency for later information, not initial information, to carry more weight than information received earlier.[2] In communication, however, immediacy and recency effects are complementary, and the presenter can utilize both. Provide your audience with a strong ending so that it will remember your presentation. It is often tempting to end a presentation with a summary of what you have presented. While this may be appropriate, remember that you may have overloaded your audience with computer information and material. Leave them with something they will remember. Once again, this serves to strengthen the communication relationship.

Blocking

In Chap. 12 we examined the idea of voice breaks to retain audience attention. *Blocking* incorporates this technique, but expands it to include the actual components of your presentation. Once you complete the outline of your speech or presentation, walk away from it for awhile. This will enable you to reexamine it later when your mind is clear. The reexamination should include blocking, which is simply the process of dividing your presentation into information blocks that are related and flow into each other. Blocking should be considered an organizational skill designed to provide you with the basis for clear organization of a presentation.

Sandwiching

The immediacy effect covers the beginning of a presentation and the recency effect covers the end of a presentation. What about the middle or body of your presentation? *Sandwiching* is a speech skill that involves presenting your strongest information at the beginning, your second strongest information at the end, and your weakest in the middle. This is the "sandwiching" presentation skill, with the slices of bread represented by the immediacy effect and the recency effect. Hopefully, you will not have any weak segments in your presentation. However, it is often necessary to provide background information with which some of your audience may already be familiar, or data that is not stimulating. Sandwiching provides you with the opportunity to present this necessary material without damaging the overall effect of the presentation.

Movement

Movement encompasses cuing and blocking. As we have discussed, cuing gives your audience clues as to the flow of your presentation, while blocking actually divides your presentation into organized, related segments. *Movement* incorporates these two speech skills, requiring the presenter to examine the presentation and bring together cuing and blocking so that it is well organized.

Types of Presentations

You can use the presentation and speech skills we've discussed in various types of presentations. Presentations can be broadly classified into two types: the unsolicited presentation and the requested presentation.

The unsolicited presentation requires you to attempt to shape your presentation to your audience without the advantage of knowing the audience's specific needs. Consequently, the problem statement discussed in the presentation strategy of *need* may be inappropriate. The unsolicited presentation is the result of your initiative. Therefore, your presentation should attempt to provide an overview of the computer subject matter. Examples of unsolicited presentations include products presentations and design and code reviews.

At the other end of the presentation spectrum is the requested presentation, better known by most of us as the "your presence has been requested" presentation. This presentation type requires you to specifically address the "open" issues, or what you are responding to in the request. Unlike the unsolicited presentation, the need has already been established. Requested presentations are often problem-oriented because the presentation is designed to provide a solution to the problem. Accordingly, you must focus your presentation on problem-solving, and provide your audience with the presentation strategy of *satisfaction*. As discussed under that presentation strategy, you must meet head-on any concerns before they crystallize. Your ability to provide answers to specific problems can often evolve into a requested presentation.

Presentation Preparation

In Chap. 11, "Writing Effective Business Letters," we discussed the importance of preparation work before the draft writing of business letters can begin. The presentation and speech skills discussed there are only effective if they are combined with the most important component of an effective and successful presentation: *Preparation*. Preparation for presentations means that you must know and understand your material inside out. Your presentation materials, discussed in the Chap. 14, are effective visual aids only to the extent that you can communicate their intended meaning. You accomplish this by knowing your material.

Your presentation often will use primary and backup material. Your ability to communicate your intended message from this material will depend on your own understanding of both. You cannot effectively communicate your message to your audience if you have not prepared it thoroughly.

Presentation Tips

As you will note from the previous section, presentations can vary greatly. There are, however, some basic presentation tips you should keep in mind, regardless of the method you choose.

Avoid placing blame

What our mothers taught us as children holds true for presentations: Do not point your finger and blame someone else. Even in cases where blame could be placed on an individual or a group for a problem or a delay, doing so could backfire on you. For example, if your presentation involves a briefing as to why a code development is late, avoid placing blame. The person you single out might later be someone you must rely on for information or help in solving the problem.

Matching information to audience knowledge

We have repeatedly emphasized the importance of recognizing the knowledge level of the person or persons who receive your communication. Employing the audience reference speech skill gives you the ability to correctly match your presentation information to your audience's background. This is especially relevant in presentations, where you do not want to talk above or below the audience's knowledge level of the computer subject matter. It would probably not be a good idea to discuss bits and bytes with the vice president of a computer software company. The material you disseminate must match the audiences' knowledge level if the audience is to remain interested in your presentation. Remember, your presentation is designed to provide useful and insightful information to your audience.

Confidence

Your confidence level will be revealed to your audience by your combined verbal and nonverbal skills. Throughout your presentation you will be attempting to establish your credibility, one of the eight speech skills discussed in this chapter. To establish your credibility you must show confidence. You must believe in yourself and believe in your presentation; the lack of confidence is often at the root of the unsuccessful presentation. The time to question yourself or your presentation is in the distant past. Now you must exude confidence, achieve the needed credibility, and the result will be a successful presentation.

Previewing the presentation location

Your confidence level will be enhanced greatly if you have the opportunity to preview the presentation room. Intangible items, such as lighting, ventilation, electrical outlet locations, and seating arrangements, can distract you and break your concentration on the presentation itself. The time you spend making yourself comfortable with these factors will give you the confidence to proceed effectively.

Summary

Employing the presentation and speech skills we have presented gives you the ability to communicate effectively with your audience. Remember, you can choose selectively from those skills that are most appropriate for a given presentation or speech. However, if you at least examine all of them you strengthen the foundation of your communication.

End Notes

1. E. R. Hilgard, R. L. Atkinson, and R. C. Atkinson, *Introduction to Psychology,* 7th ed., Harcourt Brace Jovanovich, New York, 1979.
2. Ibid.

14

Teaching
Technical Classes

At various points in their careers, many computer professionals find themselves teaching some type of technical class. This might be an evening computer science course at a local college or university, an in-house training session for a new software package, or a three-day seminar on a leading-edge technology. Each of these kinds of technical classes has its own peculiarities and distinctions, which requires the person charged with the instruction to thoroughly understand the best way to present the material to the intended audience.

This chapter will explore the different types of technical classes, and discuss their similarities as well as the differences. Nearly all of the overall verbal communications guidelines in the previous chapter, as well as the discussion of presentation materials in the next chapter, apply to teaching. When charged with this role, however, to best achieve your teaching goals you should couple that information with the information in this chapter.

We'll also talk briefly about some subjects like grading, that don't deal directly with the communications aspect of teaching technical classes. These subjects are included in this chapter in the interest of completeness with the subject matter.

Types of Technical Classes

"Teaching" can be accomplished in a number of settings. The one with which most of us are most familiar is the classroom, particularly at the 4-year college or university level (though the guidelines presented here are applicable also to high schools, junior or community colleges, or most other degree-oriented programs).

Additionally, most computer professionals have had some sort of formal training during their careers, often in programming languages, software package usage, design methodologies, or some other type of technical instruction, often conducted in house at a place of business; in many circumstances, however, it is conducted at some other location.

Let's look closely at the different settings, and discuss the distinctions between them and how to teach effectively in various settings.

College and university classes

As we mentioned above, often computer professionals teach college computer courses, usually at a local college or university. Some courses are taught by professional instructors, that is, full-time instructors or professors. Whether you are a part-time or full-time college teacher, it would be wise to follow the guidelines below.

Ordinary curriculum. By ordinary curriculum, we mean that you teach degree track undergraduate or graduate courses. While there is some overlap with adult education-oriented courses (discussed next), we make the distinction that ordinary curriculum classes are usually intended for full-time students, are longer (held over a quarter, trimester, or semester), and usually (but not always) meet several times a week.

A mistake often made by instructors in this type of setting is projecting their knowledge and experience onto the students. That is, a holder of an advanced degree in computer science with a specialization in compiler theory or operating systems often has difficulty teaching an introductory level programming or database class. Most of us have had a college instructor at one time who taught as if we were doctoral candidates rather than undergraduates in an introductory-level course. Although the explosion in personal computer technology has resulted in beginning students having more computer experience than in the past (such as when the authors attended introductory computer courses years ago), it is unlikely that many students in introductory courses have had extensive experience in computer science theory, operating systems, compiler construction, and other advanced topics. (This, of course, undoubtedly will change in upcoming years.)

On the other hand, if the attendees had been required to have taken prerequisite courses in database management systems, a graduate symposium in, for example, distributed database theory and practices, should not have its introductory lesson plan include topics such as "The Differences between Hardware and Software," or even "This Is the Relational Database Model." *The key is to gauge your audience's experience level and adjust your instruction content and style accordingly.* Nothing loses students, and results in an unpleasant experience for all (not to mention poor instructor evaluation results!) than instructing in an inappropriate framework.

Adult education. In contrast to the ordinary curriculum courses discussed above, an even greater number of computer professionals, particularly the "nonprofessional" instructors (that is, those who focus their careers primarily on the computer field in an area other than teaching and instruction), teach courses intended for working professionals. These may or may not be degree track courses. They tend to be clustered into weekend or evening adult education programs. In many circumstances adult education courses run for a relatively short period of time (typically two to six weeks) rather than over a sixteen week semester or twelve week quarter.

You might be wondering what the scheduling and orientation of these courses has to do with the instructional process. The answer is that teaching courses oriented towards working professionals *is very different* from teaching them in a traditional environment. Let's look at some distinctions, and how, if you are to be successful teaching this kind of course, you must adapt your teaching style.

1. *Consecutive classroom time.* While there are evening, one-day-per-week courses in some traditional university curricula, most are held two or three times a week, for 50 to 90 minutes. For that duration there is little or no problem with issues such as attention span. In most adult education settings, however, classes are at least three hours long, and often longer if they are taught on weekends. *It is difficult for any instructor to hold his or her students' attention consistently, week after week, for hours on end.* Your lesson plans should include appropriate breaks, changes in topic, and other tricks of the trade designed to help keep students interested for long time periods.

2. *Assignments.* Theoretically, assignments should not differ between, say, a COBOL programming course taught in a semester-long format and the same course taught in an adult education setting. In reality, though, it is difficult to give a class in the latter environment programming assignments that should take seven to ten weeks to complete, when the course is only five weeks long. Though many adult education programs offer series of courses, one after another, in the same subject (example: COBOL I through COBOL IV, each five weeks long), there is no guarantee or requirement that all students attend each and every class in the sequence, so a programming assignment in a class in COBOL I can't be carried over to a due date during the COBOL IV class. The problem is even greater in some settings where two consecutive weekends are used for a complete course; it is virtually impossible for a student who sits in a class for eight hours on a Satur-

day to prepare an assignment for the next classroom meeting, which happens to be the next day!

The point is that many instructors who are accustomed to teach in traditional environments have difficulty in adapting to teach in adult education settings, and particularly in matters such as setting appropriate assignments. It is often tempting to provide a series of simplistic assignments for these settings, but that not only is a great disservice to the students' learning processes, but also risks losing the accreditation of the university or college. Assignments should still be challenging and designed to help students learn, but should be adapted to the scheduling constraints of the particular environments. Additionally, group projects can be extremely difficult for the attendees, and, given the dispersed nature of everyone's primary job responsibilities and the limited time available for such assignments, should be considered carefully before they are assigned.

3. *Grading.* In most traditional educational courses—those, say, twelve to sixteen weeks long—it is relatively easy to compose a grading mix of quizzes, homework, programming assignments, several tests, and other components that gives students many opportunities to achieve the best grades possible. In adult education programs, with the accompanying shorter course duration, the number of items on which grades are based is significantly reduced, often to the point where one test and one or two programming assignments are the only factors in students' grades. While in theory there should be no distinction between these two sets of circumstances (certain percentages assigned to grading items and an average for each student calculated), adult education environments often wind up in an "everyone gets a good grade unless they really screw up" atmosphere, particularly in courses that span only a weekend or two.

Additionally, in a semester-long course an instructor can look at intangibles such as improvement over the duration of the course, steady attendance at "help labs" or other study sessions, and other factors that can contribute more to a student's grade than just the raw numbers. These opportunities are greatly diminished in short-term courses.

Seminars

Most computer professionals have attended some type of seminar, often held in an off-site location and taught by an expert in a particular subject. Seminars are distinguished from training in products and technology (discussed next) in that while the latter tend to be focused around achieving a specific level of proficiency in the use of a particular product or technology, seminars are "informational" in nature, with goals that may be no more tangible than "discussing the state of the art of distributed repositories."

The first, and perhaps the most important, thing to remember if you are conducting a seminar is that by virtue of your presence behind a microphone you are expected to be "one of the world's foremost experts in [whatever the subject is]." That is, seminars usually cost big money. (See the promotional literature from seminar companies and notice the high price tags.) The attendees *demand* that the seminar instructor in, for example, systems integration be an expert in that subject. While it is not recommended that you be arrogantly overconfident before any audience, you should convey your experience in the subject matter to your audience, both explicitly (through, for example, an introductory statement that explains your extensive background in the subject matter) and implicitly through your subject matter, topics, and discussions.

Secondly, at nearly every seminar there is someone in the audience intent on demonstrating his or her own expertise in the subject, and that person typically will be the most vocal in terms of questioning (and sometimes contradicting) your material. These situations require a great deal of diplomacy, particularly if that person is, shall we say, "totally incorrect." Remember that attendees are, in effect, paying customers, and deserve the right to express their opinions and ask questions. Use tactics such as, "Let's talk about that at the break; we're running a bit behind now," to diplomatically handle such situations.

In some ways, teaching seminars is similar to teaching adult education courses for working professionals. Most of the issues we discussed above apply (except for grading and, usually, assignments), particularly keeping your audience's attention over prolonged periods of time. Later in this chapter, we'll discuss certain tips that are applicable to seminars and should be kept in mind.

Product and technology training

As we mentioned above, product and technology training typically is designed to provide the students with a specified proficiency level in the use of a product or particular technology. Such training is similar to seminars, and in fact some training may be in the form of a seminar rather than a class. This type of training, however, is more like classroom instruction, except that there is no grade given.

All of your topics and subjects, and the contents of your lesson plan, should be oriented towards achieving the stated proficiency goal. (This is true of most instruction in general, but bears explicit mention here as a reminder.) It is likely, however, that a broader mix of experience levels among students will be found in training environments than in university or college classes. Oftentimes, for example, a government contractor must require all of its employees to attend 40 hours of Ada training in order to bid their services on a specific U.S. Department of Defense contract. Some of the attendees in the training session may have had no Ada experience at all, nor have they had any object-oriented programming exposure. Others may have some basic Ada experience, but lack experience in advanced concepts such as generics and tasks. Still others may have written 40,000 lines of Ada at a previous job, and are attending only because they are required to do so. *It is the instructor's job to manage these situations as creatively as possible while still attempting to meet all attendees' needs.*

After-Class Assignments

Nearly all grade- or task-oriented instruction involves some sort of after-class work as part of the instructional process. There are several guidelines you should keep in mind when assigning work to your class. These include the following:

1. *Be clear in your instructions and directions.* Always try to remember when you write the assignment sheet that the knowledge you have with respect to the assigned task is not necessarily true of the students. Explicitly state any objectives *and grading criteria.* A colleague of ours once took a programming class in a language without strict requirements on spacing within the code. The instructor made no mention of his own strict guidelines for indentation within statements, and the student (as well as others in the class) had points deducted for using her own indentation rules.

2. *Be reasonable in your assignments.* Assignments should be challenging, yet reasonable to achieve. This is particularly true of programming assignments. Scale the difficulty of the assignments to the level of the students and the objectives of the class.

Programming

As noted above, programming assignments should be reasonable and explained clearly. It is always wise to require sufficient design material (structure charts, flow charts, and so on), as well as documentation, to promote good development practices and, if possible, to provide additional material to help you diagnose the inevitable problems some students will have with the assignments.

Study work

Choose your reading and study assignments carefully and be sure they are topical. Given the rapidly changing nature of computer technology, textbooks quickly fall behind the state of the art. Supplement any text-books with readings from recent technical papers or trade periodicals.

Grading

A quick note on grading: Be consistent. Nothing can sink future teaching opportunities faster than inconsistent or biased grading of students' assignments and overall coursework. Be absolutely sure that personal likes and dislikes do not influence your grading process.

Preparation

It should be obvious that preparation is critical to successful teaching. You should always have a written lesson plan for the session at hand, regardless of whether it is a 50-minute class at a college or an all-day technical seminar. While you don't need to stick to your schedule minute by minute, it is always beneficial periodically to check your progress versus the lesson plan.

Figure 14.1 contains a sample lesson plan for a database seminar. Note that the seminar's objective is clearly noted on the lesson plan as a reminder to the instructor to ensure that the attendees are made aware of its goals and objectives.

Teaching Guidelines

Let's end this chapter with a quick list of guidelines to follow when teaching any type of technical class. We mentioned several of the items previously, but we also introduce some new topics.

1. *Stick to the advertised subject.* One of the authors taught while in graduate school. Another graduate student was also an instructor, and was assigned to teach Management Information Systems, a business-oriented undergraduate course in systems analysis and design. For some reason, the instructor decided that he didn't want to teach systems analysis, and was more interested in teaching computer hardware architecture, a decidedly science-oriented subject and far removed from systems analysis and design. Needless to say, an entire class of students was furious and led a revolt, which caused a great upheaval in the department.

On another occasion, one of the authors attended a three-day seminar that was supposed to be on expert systems. Instead of focusing on expert systems, the instructor spent most of the time discussing his research work in a totally different area. A number of attendees, all of whom had paid (or, actually, their companies had paid) a great deal of

---

**Relational Database Management Systems:
The State of the Art**

Objective: To inform experienced database professionals about the
latest advances in relational databases and database management
systems.

9:00–9:05   Introduction

9:05–10:00   Distributed relational databases

                Cover: Location transparency
                           Global optimization
                           Serializability
                           Two-phase commit

10:00–10:30   Repositories

10:30–10:45   Break

10:45–12:00   Concepts and applications of large objects; be sure to
                cover in conjunction with object-oriented databases

12:00–1:15   Lunch

1:15–2:15   4GLs and DBMSs; be sure to cover heterogeneous
                underlying databases

2:15–2:30   Last break

2:30–4:00   Survey of major DBMS vendors and their featured
                technologies

Figure 14.1 Sample lesson plan.

money for the seminar, complained loudly to the sponsor of the seminar
about the lack of focus on the advertised subject.

Always stick to the advertised subject. Improvisation is acceptable,
and a minor change of focus is desirable if, for example, the audience
turns out to be more experienced in the subject matter than had been
anticipated. It is undesirable, however, to switch to something only re-
motely related to the original topics.

2. *Attempt to foster class participation.* Courses always go more smoothly when the class is involved. There are a number of ways to increase class participation, including encouraging people to talk about their own experiences in a particular subject.

3. *Establish rapport with your audience.* Most of the techniques discussed in the previous chapter should be employed in order to establish as close of a connection with your audience as possible.

4. *Teach at the appropriate level.* As we mentioned above, your subject matter should be tuned to the appropriate experience level of your audience, regardless of the setting.

Summary

It is important to remember that teaching is a special kind of verbal presentation. As in any verbal presentation, it is essential to follow some basic guidelines and attempt to convey appropriate information to your class. In many cases, the way you perform the teaching role can influence not only your own career success (in the area of teaching) but the career success of the attendees. They rely on *you* to provide them with critical technical and other information that they need to perform their jobs or to enhance their careers. Clearly, any teacher or instructor, regardless of the setting (college or university, seminar, training session, or some other format), has a responsibility to his or her students to do the best job possible, because many careers are affected by the performance of that job.

Chapter

15

Presentation Materials

Presentations are enhanced by the method and materials you choose. As we frequently mentioned in previous chapters, you must be flexible and adapt your communications, in this case, presentation materials, to the appropriate business situation.

When one of the authors was in graduate business school, the required capstone course on strategic policy and management was designed to bring together all facets of the various business disciplines taught during the two previous years. The final assignment was an in-depth group presentation on a specific company within an industry group. Here is the story of that presentation: "We were instructed to give a dynamic and innovative presentation. My group chose food service as the general category, and targeted a chain of Mexican restaurants. My portion of the presentation involved extensive financial analysis.

"My dilemma was how to retain the audience's attention, given the fact that the class had already listened to several other presentations. How could I be innovative while presenting financial and statistical analysis? The answer was simple: by choosing my presentation materials effectively.

"I created quite a shock wave by presenting my analysis on oversized flour tortillas. By my utilizing a package of black decal letters, the tortillas became effective presentation materials, without distracting from the actual content of the presentation."

We do not advocate using food products as presentation materials in your computer presentations; tortillas just happened to complement the analysis of the Mexican restaurant chain. Rather, this example is intended to highlight the importance of choosing effective presentation materials for your particular presentation. Creativity is important in your choice of presentation materials if a synergy exists between the materials and the actual presentation.

Purpose of Presentation Materials

In basic psychology classes we are taught that a person listening to subject matter for the first time absorbs and comprehends only 30 percent of the information; the remaining 70 percent is lost. It might be possible to reverse these percentages with effective presentation materials or visual aids. As discussed in Chap. 13, your presentation actually is a series of communication strategies that provide your audience with audio-oriented sensory information. Your presentation materials should complement your oral presentation with visual reinforcement. Combined visual and verbal presentations provides sensory stimulation for two senses. Remember, a picture is worth a thousand words. Your goal is to provide your audience with audio-visual complementary information.

Preparation of Presentation Materials

Preparing your presentation materials is as important as preparing the presentation itself. Whether flipcharts, slides, or multimedia, the material should be arranged in a logical sequence to support your presentation. Often there is a tendency when working with presentation materials to jump around in the subject matter. As with your verbal presentation, the materials should be organized into clusters of information that provide smooth transitions throughout the presentation.

One of the most commonsense but most overlooked aspects of using your materials is the interaction between you and the materials. You should never use your materials for the first time at the actual presentation; it would be obvious to your audience and would undermine your credibility. You must look comfortable with your materials and view them as an extension of the presentation itself, not as separate and distinct. Consequently, you should practice the transitions from looking at your audience, to glancing at your materials, to looking back at your audience. Your goal should be to use your materials as reference tools, but not forget that your presentation is directed to your audience and not your presentation materials. Do not make the common mistake of getting lost in the materials; you and your presentation should remain in the spotlight.

Types of Presentation Materials

There are many different types of presentation materials. The selection process you use to determine which materials to present depends on the type of presentation you are giving. Match your materials to the presentation. If it is formal, slides or multimedia probably are more appropriate than flipcharts. Another factor to consider when selecting materials is the length of your presentation. Longer presentations tend to require dynamic materials to retain the audience's attention. Multimedia materials provide the varied sensory stimulation necessary to keep your audience's interest.

The following are common forms of presentation materials. Compare their inherent strengths to determine the ones that best suit your needs.

Flipcharts

This basic presentation material is simple to prepare and easy to use. Flipcharts give you the flexibility to emphasize a particular point in your presentation by instantaneously highlighting or adding to the point at hand. Because most flipcharts are hand-drawn, it is important that the writing be large, clear, and legible. Flipcharts are most appropriate for informal, smaller presentations. The size of flipcharts usually limits your ability to use them with larger audiences.

Overhead projectors

Those overhead projectors we all endured throughout our years of education are still widely used to transmit visual material. The acetate sheets used to present the materials are the essential ingredients in successful projector use. Your ability to provide computer-generated, rather than hand-written materials on the acetate sheets greatly enhances their effectiveness. Their limitation is that it is often difficult to add to the materials you are presenting: attempting to do so often results in looking directly into a blinding light. If you want to emphasize certain points that will require you to write on the acetate sheets during the presentation, practice leaning over the projector to avoid the light shining in your eyes. Remember, your nonverbal communication skills send messages to the audience simultaneously during your presentation.

Slides

Slide projectors give you the ability to present your materials in a professional manner. Preparing quality slides, with a combination of words and graphics, takes time and organization. Technology provides an advantage if you choose this means of presenting your materials: A remote control to advance the slides enables you to move about your audience freely for direct interaction while you are presenting your materials. A disadvantage of this format is the additional equipment required; You must have a screen and projector to show the slides; also, the slides cannot be altered during the presentation if you want to emphasize a particular point. Thus, slides are "fixed" presentation materials that are not readily interactive with the presenter during the presentation.

Multimedia

Presentations with multimedia formats combine a variety of visual equipment. This format is especially appropriate for software demonstrations. You can connect a projector into your PC or workstation and project the image on your terminal onto a large screen. The resulting live demonstration is an effective visual presentation for software demonstrations. This combination of various presentation formats enables the presenter to produce an effective visual presentation.

Multimedia formats require extensive preparation because of the coordination necessary among the equipment. The presenter must organize and coordinate not only the materials, but also the equipment itself. A word of caution when using a multimedia format: Do not go overboard. Remember, the presentation materials and the format in which they are delivered should complement, not detract from, the verbal portion of your presentation. A multimedia presentation for the computer professional should not look to your audience like a rock concert. It should provide your audience with a dynamic, interactive presentation that is informative and enjoyable to attend.

Presentation Material Tips

Brevity and simplicity

The audience is being exposed to numerous stimuli in your presentation. Your goal is to capture audience attention and have it focus on your presentation materials. Accordingly, brevity and simplicity are key elements in retaining their interest. All wording should be in bullet format rather than complete sentences. As brevity is important in the wording, simplicity is essential in graphics. If your audience has to spend more than a few seconds to comprehend what a chart of graphic display is showing, your message had been lost. Remember, your goal is capturing the audience's interest and attention immediately.

Relevancy

Presentation materials are visual aids designed to reinforce your topic. Consequently, the materials must be relevant to the presentation. You should use sufficient material to interest and inform, but not overload, your audience. The material should be relevant and pertinent to the points you are communicating. Remember, presentation materials are another format in which to establish a communication relationship. Therefore, it is important that the materials be relevant so that they strengthen the communication relationship.

Matching materials to location

Your initial job is to make sure that your materials complement the actual presentation. After that, be sure to match your materials to the presentation environment. Be sure that your audience can easily view the materials you are going to present. Ascertain that by previewing the presentation room before the presentation, as discussed in Chap. 14 under "Presentation Tips." Multimedia presentations often are overwhelming in smaller rooms; for a very small audience you may need to display only a software demonstration directly on your PC or workstation. The information shown to your audience by overhead projectors is often limited by the size of the image's magnification on the screen. Therefore, be sure that members of the audience at the back of the room can see the screen image. Put yourself in your audience's place, literally, to determine if you have correctly matched the presentation materials to the presentation location.

Sample Presentation Materials

This chapter ends with some sample presentation materials, namely, slides. Please note that in the interest of space, we have not included all the slides that would actually be used in these two presentations. Rather, the slides are representative of typical briefing slides that you might use in a presentation.

Preliminary Design Review

Zip's Video Automated Rental System

A&J Consulting

February 15, 1992

1

TOPICS

√ Final Priorities: Modules

√ Design Review

√ Critical Success Factors

√ Open Issues

A&J Consulting
Presentation to Zip's Video
February 15, 1992

2

FINAL PRIORITIES: MODULES

- Block 1: Video Rental System

- Customer checkout
- Daily, monthly, and annual reports
- Inventory management

- Block 2: Employee Management System

- Payroll
- Accounting

- Block 3: Customer Assistance System

- Title lookup
- Contest system

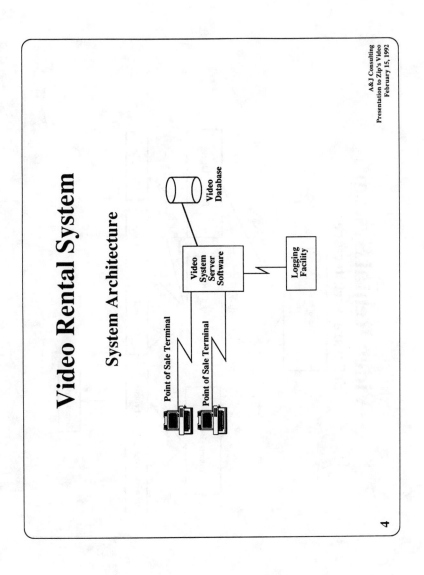

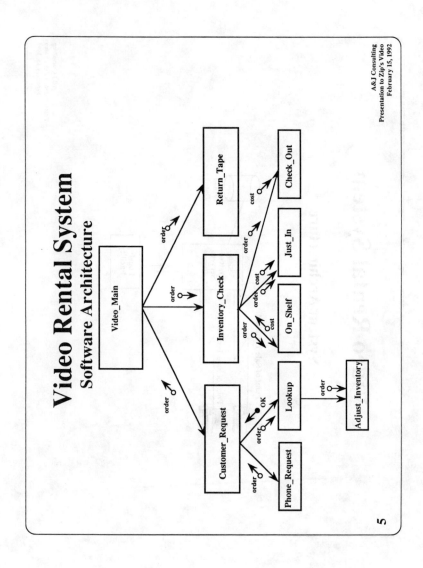

A&J Consulting
Presentation to Zip's Video
February 15, 1992

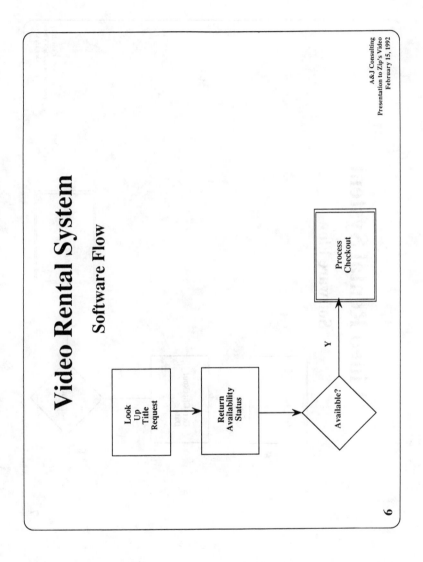

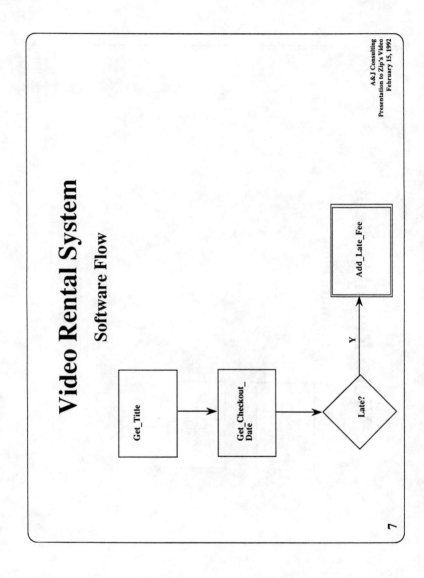

Video Rental System

Development Schedule

Item	Start Date	End Date
Design Review	Feb. 15	-
Order Hardware	Feb. 20	-
Block 1 Development	Feb. 16	April 2
Block 1 Testing	April 2	April 15
User Training	April 17	April 27
Limited Use Test	April 22	April 30

OPERATIONAL   May 1

A&J Consulting
Presentation to Zip's Video
February 15, 1992

8

Block 1 Software Development

Critical Success Factors

√ Participation of Internal Development Staff

√ Existing Cable Plant Capacity

√ User Training

√ Adherence to Schedule

A&J Consulting
Presentation to Zip's Video
February 15, 1992

9

Training Schedule

Store Location	Date
Tucson-Kolb	April 21
Tucson-Park	April 21
Phoenix-Central	April 22
Phoenix-Metro	April 23
Denver-Downtown	April 25
Colo Springs	April 26
Fort Collins	April 27

A&J Consulting
Presentation to Zip's Video
February 15, 1992

10

Development Standards

- C language programming
- Relational databases
- TCP/IP protocols
- Twisted pair connections

A&J Consulting
Presentation to Zip's Video
February 15, 1992

11

Open Issues

1. Block 2 Parallel Development

2. Heterogeneous Local Databases

3. Downtime for Systemwide Testing

4. Integration of Systems from
   Acquired Stores

A&J Consulting
Presentation to Zip's Video
February 15, 1992

12

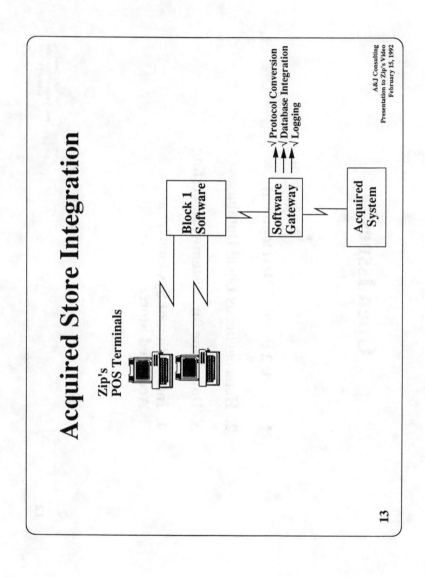

Acquired Store Integration

ISSUE: Gateway off-the-shelf or custom software?

Decision Date: NLT April 3

Owned by: Bill Jones

A&J Consulting
Presentation to Zip's Video
February 15, 1992

14

Conclusion

√ Commitment on Architecture and Design

√ Agreement on Schedule

√ Resolution of Open Issues

A&J Consulting
Presentation to Zip's Video
February 15, 1992

15

A technique you should use when conducting a presentation about a complex set of system modifications is *phased changes in slides*. Let us assume that you are describing a long-range project in which some components are gradually added and others removed over time. It is very easy for your audience to be confused about what is coming and going in terms of these components.

You can, as illustrated in the next set of slides, use shadings or, better yet, colors to highlight *gradual* changes. For example, your first slide might show some current configuration, with the components shade-coded or color-coded to indicate some significant item, such as the operational status of that system. Your next slide might show the addition of new components and interfaces, with a different coding to show that the new systems are being tested. The following slide might then show those new systems coded differently, indicating that they are now operational, and show that some of the components from your original set of slides have a changed status; and so on. Overlays are helpful if you are using overhead projector slides, or you might simply sequence your slides in a similar way as those that follow.

The important thing to remember is that it is very easy to lose your audience when presenting information about a complex sequence of changes. By your gradually and clearly showing those changes as a series of small steps, the audience will better be able to follow these modifications than if numerous changes are clustered together in your presentation materials.

Current Environment

11/92

Mainframe Customer Support

Mainframe Inventory Management

Primary Functional System

System Under Test - Backup Functional

System Under Development

Decomissioned System - Functioning as Backup

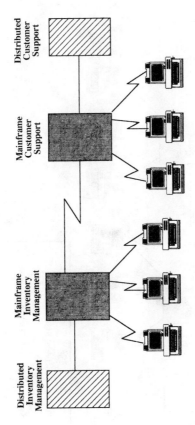

**Initial Development
1/93-8/93**

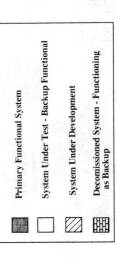

Primary Functional System

System Under Test - Backup Functional

System Under Development

Decomissioned System - Functioning
as Backup

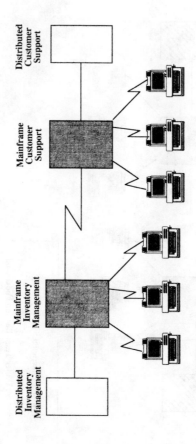

**End Phase I
Development
1/93–8/93**

Distributed Customer Support

Mainframe Customer Support

Mainframe Inventory Management

Distributed Inventory Management

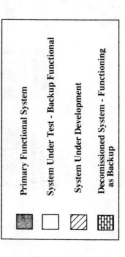

Primary Functional System

System Under Test - Backup Functional

System Under Development

Decomissioned System - Functioning as Backup

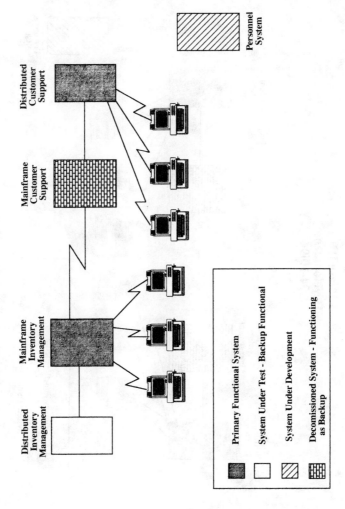

Phase II
Development
9/93-5/94

Distributed
Customer
Support

Mainframe
Customer
Support

Mainframe
Inventory
Management

Distributed
Inventory
Management

Personnel
System

Primary Functional System

System Under Test - Backup Functional

System Under Development

Decomissioned System - Functioning
as Backup

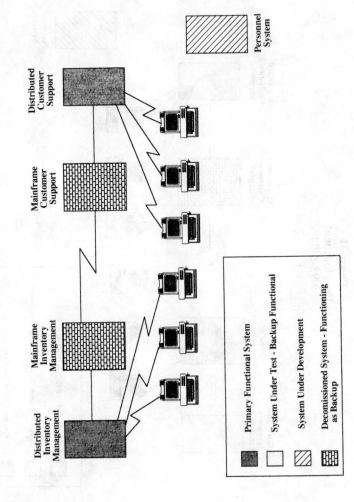

Phase III
Development
6/94-10/94

Personnel
System

Distributed
Customer
Support

Mainframe
Customer
Support

Mainframe
Inventory
Management

Distributed
Inventory
Management

Primary Functional System

System Under Test - Backup Functional

System Under Development

Decomissioned System - Functioning
as Backup

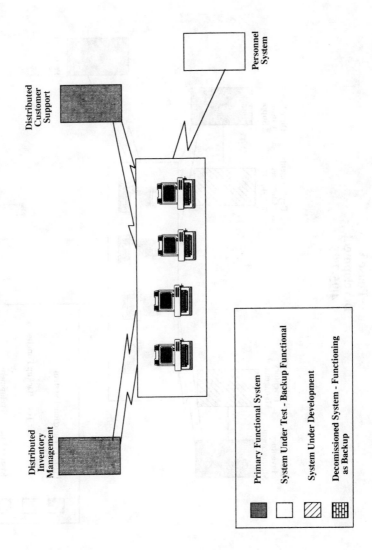

Phase IV
Development
11/94-3/95

Distributed Customer Support

Personnel System

Distributed Inventory Management

Primary Functional System

System Under Test - Backup Functional

System Under Development

Decomissioned System - Functioning as Backup

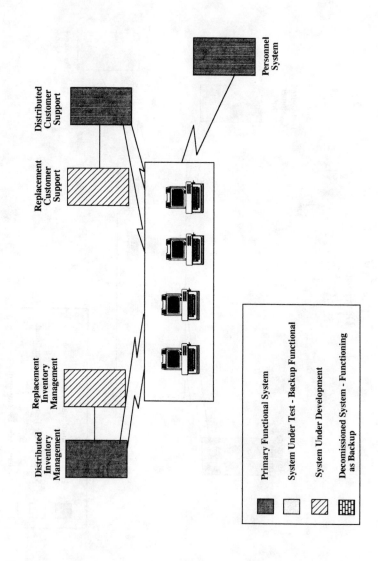

Phase V
Development
4/95-7/95

Distributed Inventory Management

Replacement Inventory Management

Replacement Customer Support

Distributed Customer Support

Personnel System

Primary Functional System

System Under Test - Backup Functional

System Under Development

Decomissioned System - Functioning as Backup

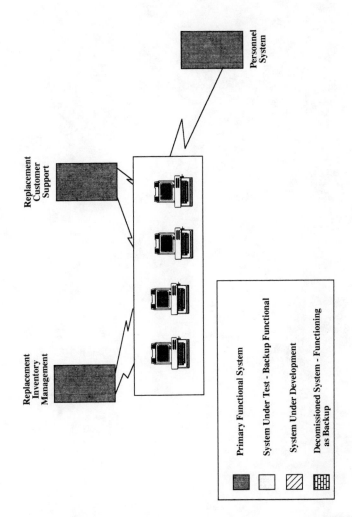

Index

ABOUT THE AUTHORS

ALAN R. SIMON is a full-time freelance writer. He is the author of McGraw-Hill's *How to Be a Successful Computer Consultant* and *The Computer Professional's Survival Guide*. He has held a number of consulting and staff positions in the computer industry since 1979.

JORDAN S. SIMON holds an M.B.A. from the University of Southern California and a B.S. in Business Administration from the University of Arizona. He has previously published several freelance articles.